ACADEMIC DEBATE: PRACTICING ARGUMENTATIVE THEORY

SECOND EDITION

by
Donald W. Klopf
and
Ronald E. Cambra
University of Hawaii

Morton Publishing Company
2700 East Bates Ave
Denver, Colo 80210

Contents

Preface

Academic Debate: Practicing Argumentative Theory provides guided learning for students who want to test their speaking skills in the competitive atmosphere of the debate tournament. The theory of argumentation covered in the book has a practical bent. It is designed to prepare the students for academic debating and written with the hope that those who debate successfully using the academic style will speak equally as well in real life — at work, at home, at play, in the law court, in the legislative assembly, wherever democracy is at work.

Those who do debate participate in an ancient endeavor. Academic or school debate has provided training in oral communication for students for two thousand years, and it is believed to be the most potent force today in the speech training of students throughout the world. Debate contests are carried on by high school and university students in virtually every literate society in which free speech is permitted.

The popularity of academic debate seems directly related to the benefits derived by those who participate. Debaters do become skillful oral communicators, not only in speaking before large audiences but also as communicators in small groups of two or more people.

A debate book, however, plays only a part in becoming a skillful oral communicator. Practice under the guidance of an expert speech teacher or coach is needed. The tournament experience with the critic-judge on hand to give additional help is also necessary. Nonetheless, for those who use it well, much value will be gained from the fundamentals offered by a debate book.

This edition of *Academic Debate: Practicing Argumentative Theory* contains new material. The chapter on the argumentative process develops the theory more fully. Sections on speaker duties have been added to the chapters on the affirmative and negative cases. The cross-questioning chapter, we believe, now represents a more adequate treatment of the questioning process, perhaps better than that found in other debate texts. Finally, a judging chapter gives debaters an understanding of why and how decisions are rendered. Hopefully, this explanation will reduce the gripes about debate judging.

As in the original edition, our aim has been simplicity. We have sought to cover the fundamentals clearly without embellishment, feeling that to debate the student should know about the process but not every detail.

This book draws some of its material from several sources which should be acknowledged. *The Bases of Debate* by Donald Klopf and Takehide Kawashima (Tokyo: Sansyusya Publishing Co., 1977) is foremost among these. The article, "The State of the Affirmative Case," by Donald Klopf, *Communication, the Journal of the Communication Association of the Pacific,* Volume IV, June 1976, Number 2, forms the basis for the affirmative case description. The article, "In Defense of the Status Quo: Strategies for Dealing with Proposals for Change in Public Policy Advocacy," by James Benjamin, *Communication, the Journal of the Communication Association of the Pacific,* Volume VI, July 1977, Number 2, is the source of much of the negative case material. The information on unfavorable debate practices comes from the article, "Ethical Practices in Contemporary Debate," by Donald Klopf, *Communication, the Journal of the Communication Association of the Pacific,* Volume V, July 1976, Number 1. Some of the material on questioning is based on that in *Interviewing* (San Jose, Ca.: Lansford Publishing Co., in press) and *Cross-Examination Debate* (Tokyo: Gaku Shobo Publishing Co., 1978) by Donald Klopf. Excerpts from *Judging Speech Contests* (Tokyo: Gaku Shobo Publishing Co., 1978) and *Coaching and Directing Forensics,* revised (Skokie, Ill.: National Textbook Co., in press) by Donald Klopf, are included in Chapter 10.

Donald W. Klopf
Ronald E. Cambra

Honolulu, Hawaii

1

Academic Debating

Living is largely a matter of communicating. The professor lectures to his pupils; the pupil converses with his friends; the customer asks the clerk about the article she wants to purchase; the lawyer defends his client; the mother praises her child. They are all communicating. People communicate from morning to night, particularly in a modern industrial society like ours where most people make their living communicating. Some people are professional communicators. Teachers, actors, lawyers, ministers fall into this group. Others also make their living communicating, as salesmen, policemen, legislators, government officials, and businessmen of all sorts. More than twenty thousand different ways of earning a living exist in modern society, and oral as well as written communication is essential to every one. When communication is not a vital part of the job, it is still an essential part of life. We socialize with our friends and neighbors, attend classes, participate in community groups, shop for food, express our choices for elected office. Communication is inseparable from life.

Communication takes various forms, one of which is a primary concern of speech education — oral communication. But in all forms the ultimate purpose of the communicator is to be understood, to communicate so that those to whom he communicates comprehend what he says. His goal is to convey his message so clearly to his receivers that they will respond in the manner he desires. Speech education aims at accomplishing this goal, as students in the classroom become familiar with the fundamentals of oral communication.

The extra-curricular experiences provided by debate also fulfill the purpose of working toward improved communication. But debate has features which make it more valuable than classroom training. Debate confronts the student participant with circumstances more like real life as he speaks to persuade an audience to his point of view. In addition, debate emphasizes critical evaluations of performance and supplies suggestions for improvement from expert judges.

For our purposes, debate consists of the advocative events that are organized as contests between teams of students. Contests between teams involve several people working and speaking together on one side of the competition. Debate is such a contest since it usually requires four students split into two teams, or sides, with one team of two defending the debate proposition and another team of two urging rejection of that proposition.

On the other hand, there are contests between individual speakers which are called the "individual" events. They are so called because they involve one student, an individual, who prepares and speaks by himself. He may speak in a contest with several other students, however, he speaks as an individual and is judged as an individual. The two major types of "individual" contests are public speaking and interpretative reading contests. If the student creates the material of the speech he delivers from his own experience and research, he is engaged in public speaking. If he reads aloud and orally interprets the material of others, he is engaged in interpretative reading.

The Nature of Academic Debate

Debate involves oral or written communication over the important economic, social, political, and philosophical issues of a society and takes place only in those societies in which the people have some responsibility for making decisions. In an authoritarian system of government, led by a powerful few who perpetuate themselves in office by force, threats, or coercion, the people can neither meaningfully nor safely debate against the government's position on the vital problems of the society. By contrast, in our governmental system, the people have a voice in what the society does. The people elect their fellow citizens to represent them, and these representatives are expected to be responsive to the needs and desires of those who elected them.

If our representative form of government is to work, its citizens must express their opinions about the nation's problems. Debate becomes a key tool in stating ideas effectively since debate, as we define it, is competitive advocacy, for or against an issue, occurring without limitations of time, place, or form.

Competitive advocacy means to argue for one side of a problem against someone who argues for the other side of the same problem. Communication of this sort happens in a variety of settings — in Congress, in the courtroom, in the classroom, and even in our homes. These varied settings permit us to classify debate into two major groups — substantive or real-life debate and academic or educational debate.

Substantive debate is that form of competitive advocacy we partake of when we argue with parents, friends, classmates, and business associates about the daily problems of our ordinary life. It also is that competitive advocacy in which lawmakers, lawyers, businessmen, philosophers, and others engage during their normal work day. In contrast, academic debate is that form of competitive advocacy conducted as contests by high schools and universities for students who want the training necessary to become more effective substantive debaters.

In order to give those who participate the maximum educational instruction, academic debate follows consistent patterns of speaking behavior, unlike substantive debate. Teams, affirmative and negative, are formed to debate a proposition which is written so that each team defends an opposing side of the proposition and each team must consistently defend its side as the debate unfolds. A team cannot change or reverse its position once the position is stated.

This consistent maintenance of opposed viewpoints is done for the sake of argument. Both affirmative and negative speakers agree to maintain their position so that the arguments of both sides receive the undivided attention of the debaters and each side tries to present every available bit of evidence and reasoning on its side in the best possible manner.

The development of academic debate into well-defined forms has made possible the tremendous growth of inter-school tournament debate in the United States. Many debates can be conducted in a short period of time. The average debate runs about an hour, and, in an eight-hour tournament, a team may debate in as many as eight debates. Of course, a great deal of speaking experience comes from so much debate and the educational values are immeasurable.

Academic debate's procedures, therefore, permit those students who take part to learn how to argue more effectively so that when they do engage in real-life or substantive debate, they will interact more successfully. Although much of the substantive debate we partake of follows few of the rules or regulations of academic debate — debate in the court of law or legislative chambers is an exception — we are able to hone our speaking skills in academic debate because of the procedures that allow maximum participation.

Orthodox Debate.

The form most frequently debated is "orthodox" debate, sometimes referred to as "standard," "traditional," or "oxford-style" debate. In this format the affirmative team of two members and a negative team of the same number compete under fixed rules to argue a stated resolution. The debate normally is judged by one or more critics who render a decision at the debate's completion. The decision indicates what team did the better debating and the team judged best is declared the "winner."

The opening speaker of what is usually an hour-long debate is the first affirmative. The first negative follows, and the second affirmative and second negative alternate next to complete the "constructive" speeches. The first negative immediately begins the "rebuttal" speeches followed by the first affirmative, second negative, and second affirmative in turn. The usual time sequence:

Constructive Speeches		Rebuttal Speeches	
1. First Affirmative	10 minutes	1. First Negative	5 minutes
2. First Negative	10 minutes	2. First Affirmative	5 minutes
3. Second Affirmative	10 minutes	3. Second Negative	5 minutes
4. Second Negative	10 minutes	4. Second Affirmative	5 minutes

The orthodox format follows a procedure observed in most debate forms, that is, the affirmative team speaks first and last. The affirmative ordinarily argues for a change in the *status quo* while the negative in most debates argues for the retention of the *status quo*. The affirmative, therefore, should speak first to introduce the proposition and to explain why the *status quo* should be changed. Should the affirmative not speak first, the negative would have no reason to speak at all since they would not have an affirmative case to clash with. The affirmative closes the debate in order to summarize the reasons for changing the *status quo*.

Cross-Examination Debate.

Cross-examination debate gives the same skills training obtained in orthodox debate, and, additionally, training in the useful art of questioning opponents. This additional feature makes cross-examination debate about as popular as orthodox.

Cross-examination debate is similar to orthodox in many respects. It requires affirmative and negative teams to speak for and against a proposition and, as they do so, they must follow the identical procedures of the orthodox form. Cross-examination differs in that questioning periods follow each of the constructive speeches. In these periods an opponent questions the preceding constructive speaker. He does this to clarify vague ideas, to disclose faulty reasoning or errors in evidence, and to secure admissions that could damage the opposition's case.

The questioning periods can be seen in this cross-examination time format.

1. First affirmative constructive speech — 8 minutes

2. First affirmative questioned by second negative — 3 minutes

3. First negative constructive speech — 8 minutes

4. First negative questioned by first affirmative — 3 minutes

5. Second affirmative constructive speech — 8 minutes

6. Second affirmative questioned by first negative — 3 minutes

7. Second negative constructive speech — 8 minutes

8. Second negative questioned by second affirmative — 3 minutes

9. First negative rebuttal — 4 minutes

10. First affirmative rebuttal — 4 minutes

11. Second negative rebuttal — 4 minutes

12. Second affirmative rebuttal — 4 minutes

A variety of cross-examination formats have been developed but in the one above, each speaker defends his ideas under the cross-questioning of an opponent, thus, each speaker gains questioning experience as he cross-questions an opponent. In other formats, not every speaker gets a chance to question.

Debating's History

Educational debate in the West began at least 2400 years ago when the scholar Protagoras of Abdera (481-411 B.C.), known as the "father of debate," conducted debates among his students in Athens and Sicily, city-states in the Mediterranean Sea area now called Greece. In that time, other teachers of rhetoric also taught their students debate, particularly so that they might plead their own cases in the law courts.

Aristotle (384-322 B.C.) laid the foundation for modern argumentation and debate in his famous book, *The Rhetoric,* which in its translated English version is still widely read. The book largely was responsible for installing rhetoric into ancient and medieval universities as one of the liberal arts.

During the first 1400 years of recorded Western history after the birth of Christ, speech education in all forms flourished or perished along with a person's freedom of speech. When people enjoyed the freedom to speak freely, speech training blossomed. When the rulers prohibited free speech, speech training lay dormant.

By the early 1400's medieval Europe provided an atmosphere conducive to the growth of speech education and about that time the first contest debate between two schools took place. Oxford met Cambridge at Cambridge in what seems to be the start of debates between schools. This debate and those that followed usually were conducted in Latin, in the form of technical disputes over abstract points of law.

The American colonial colleges transported European debate to the New World where disputation was made part of the curriculum and a featured part of commencement ceremonies.

Debate as we now know it owes its existence to the American college literary societies of the eighteenth century, the earliest of which was the Spy Club founded at Harvard in 1722. The Spy Club promoted debate and rebelled against the legal technical disputes imported from Europe. And, Harvard supposedly debated Yale, January 14, 1892, at Cambridge, in what some believe was the "first modern intercollegiate debate," although other contests preceded it.

During the first decade of their development in the United States, intercollegiate debate contests were negotiated by the opposing schools. Rules of procedure, the topic to be debated, judge selection, finances, and so forth were arranged by the students involved. However, another ten years saw the establishment of leagues, stabilization of procedures, and the emergence of contest activity as an integral part of most school's curriculum. Today hundreds of thousands of high school and college students under the guidance of trained speech educators engage annually in debate contests all over America.

We estimate that over 300 major intercollegiate contests and an estimated 500 interscholastic league contests are held annually with approximately fifteen schools and fifty students on the average taking part in each contest, and we expect our estimates are the minimum. No known record of the number of intra-school meets or non-league interscholastic contests exists, but thousands undoubtedly occur each year.

Debate's Rewards

That debate training benefits those who participate seems evident from what we have said so far. Certainly the phenomenal growth of debate attests to its educational value. Hundreds of thousands of students around the world have partaken of debate, and interest appears to be growing in many countries. Debate provides the participant with a variety of practical educational experiences that few other forms of education give.

Research studies show debate's educational values. The evidence from carefully planned studies supports these conclusions: (1) debaters and those who study argumentation improve significantly in their ability to think critically; (2) success in debate ranks next to scholarship in attaining success in business and industry; and (3) learning in most all areas of study increases significantly as a result of debate activity.

Perhaps more important that these research conclusions are the testimonials to the value of debate training from those who participated. The debate literature abounds with survey reports in which those sampled testified overwhelmingly in behalf of the value of their own debate experiences.

In America a large body of men and women established for themselves nationwide reputations as impressive speakers. Congressmen, legislators in local governments, lawyers, teachers, businessmen, and numerous other outstanding citizens are among many who have acknowledged the values of their speech training. A summary of their comments suggests that the debater learns:

To use oral communication in a socially responsible way, and thus become a more effective member of his society.

To become a more able person, and thus reveal a more stable and mature personality.

To speak and read with clear purpose, and thus avoid meaningless talk.

To develop an appreciation of and a knowledge about worthwhile original speech subjects.

To do intelligent research in finding materials as well as to develop skill in creative, rational thinking.

To analyze and adapt to various speaking situations.

To organize material in a meaningful way for communication with an audience.

To use voice effectively in the communication of ideas and feelings.

To use bodily action purposefully in the act of communication.

To use language more effectively by phrasing ideas into direct, clear, and impressive language.

To conclude, the participant in academic debate learns to speak more satisfactorily in his daily contacts with friends and associates. As a result, he becomes a more productive and responsible member of his society.

2

The Debate Proposition:
Its Form and Analysis

Before an academic debate can begin, the participants must first mutually agree upon the proposition to be debated. The proposition in academic debate almost always is a proposition of "policy." That is, it is a statement that something should be done — that some new policy of action should be adopted to change the present situation. Here are three propositions of policy: "Resolved: That the United States should adopt a permanent program of price and wage controls; Resolved: That the powers of the Presidency should be curtailed; Resolved: That the federal government should adopt a comprehensive program to control land use in the United States."

Note that each of the resolutions contains several elements:
1. An agent to do the acting — in the example, "the United States should adopt . . . ," "United States" is the agent.
2. The verb "should" — in a proposition of policy, *should* implies that the action suggested by the proposition is *possible* to carry out, not that it *will* be carried out. Debaters only need to show that the proposed action is possible; it is not necessary to prove that people will actually take the action.
3. An active verb to complete the "should" verb combination — in the example, ". . . should *adopt* . . ."
4. The action desired — in the example, ". . . a permanent program of wage and price controls," which is a new policy changing the present situation or *status quo*.

When framing propositions for debate the four elements stated above have to be included and essentials should be met: (a) the proposition should be truly controversial; (b) it must place the burden of proof on the affirmative and the presumption on the negative; (c) it should be of interest to the audience and suit the occasion; and (d) it should include only one subject. Should the proposition read, "Resolved: That Japan and the United States should adopt a permanent program of wage and price controls," then two subjects, Japan and the United States, would be included and the proposition would not be debatable since economic conditions in the two countries are different.

Students who engage in contest debate are not concerned with proposition wording, since contest debates use propositions framed by national committees. The national propositions are debated for the duration of an academic year and are used in almost every contest or tournament debate held throughout the nation.

Two different propositions are debated, one by the high schools and the other by the universities. Both propositions are prepared by committees in roughly the same fashion. At a previously agreed upon time, each committee polls debate coaches for debate topic suggestions, the high school committee polls high school coaches, and the university committee, university coaches. The coaches' suggestions are worded into propositions by the committees and sent back to the coaches for a vote. The propositions receiving the most votes become the debate propositions for the academic year.

The practice of using one proposition at the high school level and another at the university level largely accounts for the great numbers of tournament debates. All a debate team needs to do in order to enter almost any tournament is to prepare one debate proposition, rather than prepare a different one for every tournament. Thus, preparation can be thorough with the average debater becoming an expert in the subject.

Many debaters participate in debates before audiences, in addition to tournament debates, and in their audience debates, they frequently use propositions different than the national ones. Through this practice, they get to prepare more than one proposition, thus, they gain more research experience.

Proposition Analysis

Debate preparation is concerned primarily with discovering appropriate arguments and securing adequate evidence to support the arguments in order to assemble them into affirmative or negative cases. The first task in preparation, therefore, is to discover the appropriate arguments, and to do this, the debater analyzes the proposition.

There are two main reasons for analyzing the proposition. First, it must be thoroughly analyzed in order to determine what the affirmative and negative issues are likely to be in the debate. When these are known, we will have the basic ingredients of affirmative and negative cases. In addition, when we thoroughly analyze the proposition, we are not likely to overlook arguments that will strengthen our case. Similarly, we are much less likely to be surprised by an argument that our opponents present. Should our analysis be incomplete, unsystematically conducted, or terminated too soon, our case will probably be weaker than it could be and we will be more vulnerable to attack by a better prepared opponent.

Second, we must thoroughly analyze the proposition to determine what issues to research. Knowing the issues, we then can systematically investigate the available literature relating to each of the issues. We do this to uncover the relevant evidence required to prove the arguments, or to refute those of the opposition. Instead of randomly searching for evidence, our research should have direction and a goal.

Steps in Analysis

How is the debate proposition analyzed? First, we must analyze the terms of the proposition by defining them. Then, we can use one of two models to conduct our analysis. Either the stock issues model or the systems model can be used, both of which have merits depending upon the nature of the resolution.

Defining the Terms of the Proposition.

Propositions are intended to clearly state the basis for dispute. However, should the proposition not be understood to mean the same thing by both the affirmative and negative, no meaningful debate can take place. Occasionally, in a debate, both sides define the terms differently, and considerable clash occurs over whose definitions are most appropriate. Terms do have multiplicity of meaning and care must be exercised in analysis to arrive at mutually agreeable and fitting definitions in order to reduce or eliminate unnecessary wrangling over terms.

The "terms" are not always the individual words in the proposition. Usually the terms consist of several words grouped into meaningful phrases, as in this example (the terms are set off by slash lines): Resolved:

That/ the sale of/ pornographic literature/ should be/ prohibited/ in America.

Not every term needs to be defined. You need only to define those which appear to have more than one meaning. Many terms hold only one meaning and need not be defined. For example, the term "should" always holds the same meaning. Others may require definition as in the proposition cited above. In that proposition, "sale," "pornographic literature" and "prohibited" should be defined since each has several possible interpretations. The other terms, however, seem self-explanatory.

There are numerous ways to define terms, however, debaters usually use authority, illustration, synonym, and negation.

The most frequently employed way is by authority, that is, to use an expert source like the dictionary, encyclopedia, or recognized scholarly book on the subject. The ordinary dictionary has limitations, however, so that you should keep in mind the total context of the debate proposition in which the word appears. Dictionaries define single words. Debate terms often appear as phrases expressing legal, political, economic, or social meanings not given in most dictionaries. "Pornographic literature" is a term with legal and social implications which the average dictionary does not include. In a scholarly book that deals with the subject matter of pornography, a more appropriate definition undoubtedly will be stated.

A way that is often effective for defining a term is to cite an illustration known to the audience. To illustrate, on the resolution, "Resolved: That Puerto Rico should establish a guaranteed minimum hourly wage for all industrial workers," the affirmative could define the resolution by saying, "by a 'guaranteed minimum hourly wage' we mean a system similar to that currently in operation elsewhere in the fifty United States."

Often the meaning of a term can be defined by substituting synonyms for the words in it. For example, the term, "a guaranteed minimum hourly wage" may be better understood by replacing it with another expression meaning the same thing, such as "assured hourly income."

Occasionally the meaning of a term may be defined by negation — explaining what is not. In the resolution, "Resolved: That the United States should prohibit the sale of marijuana to those under eighteen years of age," we would be defining what we mean by "under eighteen years of age" using negation if we would say something like "by under eighteen years of age we do not mean those people who have already observed their eighteenth birthday."

Who should define terms in a debate? The responsibility is that of the affirmative and the first affirmative debater in particular. The negative team assumes the right to accept or reject the definitions, and offer their own if they believe the affirmative's to be inaccurate or unfair and the first negative speaker normally accepts or rejects the terms for the negative side.

The affirmative is honor bound to use fair and reasonable definitions and should avoid tricky definitions which are used to gain a special advantage. At the same time, the negative should avoid quibbling over terms and generally should accept the definitions of the affirmative so that the debate can rightfully center on the issues.

To conclude our discussion of term definition, the first step of proposition analysis, we suggest these questions as guides in conducting an analysis of terms:

1. What are the "terms" of the proposition?

2. Which terms may be misinterpreted and, hence, require definition?

3. What are good ways of defining such terms?

4. What are fair and reasonable definitions for such terms?

5. Are there any terms not stated in the proposition that may occur in the debate that need definition? If so, what are fair and reasonable definitions for them?

Issues Analysis.

What are the issues in a debate? The issues may be defined as "those critical questions, inherent within the proposition, upon whose answers the acceptance or rejection of the proposition rests." This definition states that issues are questions which should be answered by both the affirmative and negative in order to decide if the proposition should, or should not, be accepted. The questions are phrased so that the affirmative team answers "yes" to each and the negative "no."

Each debate proposition involves a set of issues of its own which would be impossible to discuss in a sensible fashion apart from the proposition. However, it is possible to examine some common characteristics of all debate propositions which tend to be the same regardless of the subject matter of the proposition. These common characteristics, or common issues, are called "stock issues," and they are helpful in finding the issues in any debate proposition.

There are five stock issues and both the affirmative and negative teams can defend their position on the basis of the five issues.

1. Is there a problem in existence which needs to be solved? Before the average person alters the *status quo* or the way he normally does something, he usually has to be convinced that the *status quo* either is faulty and presently is causing difficulties, or, in the future, it will be

faulty and cause difficulties. To uncover the answers to this stock issue requires a study of the present system including its history. Such a study should reveal the problems with the present, if any, and why they occurred.

The following questions offer guidelines in analyzing the first stock issue: (a) How does the present system operate? (b) How did the present system start and why? (c) What is wrong with the way things are now? (d) Who is harmed by the present system? Why? (e) Why are things done the way they are? (f) Is there some reason they must continue to be done the way they are now?

Note that academic debate propositions are based on the assumption that something is wrong with the *status quo,* otherwise there would be little cause to debate. Hence, numerous reasons why the *status quo* should be changed will stem from the research. When you debate affirmatively, you choose the most potent of these reasons in building your case; when you are on the negative side, you need to know them all in order to defend the *status quo* adequately.

2. Is the problem, or its cause, an inherent part of the *status quo*? "Inherent" means existing as a natural part of a person, object, or policy. For example, the automobile is defined as a vehicle that carries its own engine and is used on streets and highways. The engine is an inherent part of the automobile, according to the definition of an automobile. Without the engine, the automobile would not be an automobile but merely a vehicle. So it is with the problem, or cause of the problem, in the *status quo.* The problem must exist as a natural part of the *status quo*; if it doesn't, the *status quo* would not be. The present policy is so constructed that it cannot eliminate the problem; the only way to eliminate it is to change the policy. With a policy change, the *status quo* no longer exists.

The "inherency" issue, therefore, deals with the relationship between the present problem and the present policy. Questions like the following usually help in discovering the extent of this relationship: (a) Must we adopt a new policy in order to overcome the problem? or, (b) Can we continue to practice the present policy and overcome the problem? or, (c) Can we modify the present policy in some way without adopting a new one and still overcome the problem?

Once the relationship has been established, answer these questions in order to establish inherency: (a) What caused the problem? (b) Have attempts been made in the past to solve the problem? (c) If previous attempts were made, what was their relationship to the present policy? (d) Did the previous attempts fail? If so, why? Were the failures due to structural barriers, attitudinal barriers, or what?

The presumption in academic debate is that there are no problems of consequence in the *status quo* until the affirmative proves they do exist. Therefore, the affirmative has to demonstrate that problems exist (stock issue 1) and, just as important, that these problems are inherent (stock issue 2) in the *status quo* policy.

3.   Would the action suggested in the debate resolution eliminate the inherent problem? After deciding that there is an inherent need for a change in the *status quo*, the debater needs to determine how to solve the problem. The third stock issue relates to "plan," that is, course of action, a method, or a way to remove the problem.

Analysis for the third stock issue should answer these two questions: (a) What possible plans could be suggested as means of eliminating the problems? (b) How will these plans solve the problems? By examining all possible plans, both affirmative and negative will benefit. The affirmative should come up with the best one for them and the negative should be prepared to refute every plan possibility.

4.   Is it reasonable to assume that the plan implied by the resolution could be implemented? The fourth stock issue, the "practicality" issue, questions whether or not the plan could actually be carried out. Answering these specific questions should prove helpful in determining practicality: (a) Is the plan feasible? That is, can the plan be organized administratively and financed? (b) Is the plan enforceable? That is, are there ways to enforce the plan and will these ways be effective? (c) What effects may result from the plan? Will it solve the problems? Will it remove the causes of the problem?

Through an examination of practicality, both the affirmative and negative should uncover the plan's weaknesses, if any, and the affirmative can strengthen or do away with these weaknesses. The negative, on the other hand, can debate the weaknesses if the affirmative fails to correct them.

5.   Would the affirmative plans be free from serious detrimental side effects if they were adopted? A change in the *status quo* inevitably leads to desirable and undesirable side effects. The critical point in the fifth stock issue is whether these side effects will be more desirable than undesirable. So, the debater needs to discover the advantages and disadvantages of the various plan possibilities and decide which plan is more desirable. The answers to these questions will be helpful: (a) What are the possible advantages and disadvantages of the plan? (b) Have any similar plans been tried in the past? If so, what were their effects? (c) What criteria are useful for evaluating these advantages and disadvantages? (d) Are the advantages desirable in terms of these criteria?

A thorough analysis of all possible affirmative plans should reveal the plan, or perhaps several plans, that are best for the affirmative, and at the same time, should help determine the significant arguments against all affirmative plans for the negative.

To summarize the stock issues method, we rephrase the stock issues more simply as (1) Is there a need for a change? (2) Is the need inherent? (3) Will the plan meet the need? (4) Is the plan practical? (5) Do the advantages of the plan outweigh the disadvantages?

The affirmative analysis requires a "yes" answer to each of these questions, that is, the affirmative contends: "Yes, there is a need to change the *status quo*." "Yes, the need is inherent." "Yes, there is a plan which will meet the need." "Yes, the plan is practical." "Yes, the advantages are more important than the disadvantages." When the affirmative can supply "yes" answers for the five stock questions, it has the makings of a *prima facie* case. The negative analysis on the other hand calls for "no" answers. "No," the negative argues, "there is no need for a change," and so on. Both sides, of course, attempt to prove with adequate evidence and reasoning that their side is right. However, the affirmative with proof to support its "yes" answers has constructed a defensible *prima facie* case.

Using the stock issues method, the affirmative has certain responsibilities to carry out and its case is normally developed around them. The responsibilities are: (1) show that evils or problems exist, (2) show that these evils are produced by causes that can be remedied, (3) show that the action or policy proposed provides a remedy and (4) show that this remedy is practicable in terms of cost, new problems it might create, and other possible remedies. For quick reference these may be referred to as "ill," "blame," "cure," and "cost."

Systems Analysis.

Another model of analysis deserves attention — the systems model. It assumes a complexity of actions and conditions which are interrelated to numerous other actions and conditions within the socio-political framework of public policy. This complexity is characterized by *multiple causation, equifinality,* and *multiple effects.*

Multiple causation rejects the belief that one factor may be isolated as the cause of another. Instead, there are a number of simultaneously occurring conditions which contribute to an extremely complex causal relationship. A socio-political problem, for example, could involve an exigency, the attitudes of those who make public policy or who implement such policies, and the structure under which those individuals operate. To illustrate, each New Year's Eve dozens of Honolulu residents are injured by exploding firecrackers. A law banning fireworks would eliminate the problem. In order to pass the law, its proponents would have to consider the multiple factors that come to play in this situation. The exigency itself is a factor. Also important is the attitude of the largely Oriental population which considers exploding firecrackers a significant religious, cultural, and historical way of celebrating certain occasions. The political and law enforcement structures in Honolulu are also critical. The politicians draw votes from the Orientals; many are Oriental and attach importance to the use of fireworks. Likewise, many of the police are Oriental and may be inclined to overlook infractions of a fireworks ban. They may simply be too busy on New Year's Eve with more serious violations of the law. As a consequence of these multiple factors, Honolulu has failed to ban fireworks.

Equifinality, the second characteristic, assumes that a number of different causal complexes can have identical effects. Inflation, for instance, can result from a number of complex causal relationships — supply and demand, labor-management negotiations, and inflationary psychology, to name a few. Any one of these causal systems, however, may in itself create inflation.

The *multiple effects* characteristic suggests that any one change in a system will effect other relationships within that system. Banning fireworks in Honolulu will result in an economic hardship for fireworks' sellers, will alter ceremonial procedures in many religions, and will add to the police's burden.

Such a system for analyzing public policy isolates these points of judgment: "(1) the alternative courses of action open or available within ones influence, (2) the likely effects of pursuing each of the alternatives, (3) the probability of the various effects, (4) the value of each effect, and (5) the attitude toward risk and probability." Thus, the single dominant cause relationship argument of the traditional model is replaced by a model which accommodates multiple causality, suggesting many alternatives with many effects. These are related by probability arguments and sorted by arguments comparing advantages and disadvantages. Consideration is also given to the priority of goals because of the value of effects. Multiple effects imply a trade-off among goals and the values must be weighed.

The stock issues model uses the concept of *prima-facie* case as a standard by which debaters argue, making the acceptance or rejection of the *status quo* critical early in the debate. The systems model makes the critical judgment additive and comparative with the policy judgment a final step. The policy alternatives will have many effects. Judgment follows, first, the assessment of the probability and value of each effect for each alternative and, next, the weighing of these against the effects of the other alternatives including that of the *status quo*. This weighing argument allegedly replaces the inherency argument vital to the traditional case.

The weighing process is where the five points of judgment in the systems model merge in the critical process. The key to weighing is impact, which advances three principles: (1) other things being equal, the greater the probability of the policy options generating the effect, the greater the impact; (2) other things being equal, the greater the significance of the effect generated by the alternative, the greater the impact; and (3) other things being equal, the more important the goal or value involved, the greater the impact. Argument will take place over probability, significance, and value, then center on the total comparative impact of advantages and disadvantages of various policy options.

To sum up, the systems model views debate as consisting of the comparison of policy systems. "Comparison" in the systems model means that the affirmative and negative argue for some policy or policies and the winner is the one whose policy is best among those being compared. "System" implies that the policy arrangements being compared are typically complex, multifaceted, and interrelated entities that are defined not only statically by their structure but dynamically by their goals, behavior, and interactions.

3

Research in Academic Debate

Academic debate propositions require a great deal of reading and research before they can be analyzed with thoughtfulness. Also, before the debater can gather and organize evidence to build a case, he has to be knowledgeable about the proposition. Thus, much of what is done in academic debate revolves around research. Proposition analysis, collecting evidence, case construction, rebuttal and refutation preparation, all demand research. Proposition analysis especially depends upon research. The stock issues model, for example, gives direction to research. The material uncovered in research reveals the debate's true issues. Each is dependent upon the other, as in the other activities like evidence gathering, case construction, and so on.

Analysis and research continue throughout the debate season. They are not completed after a few weeks of work and then ignored for the balance of the year. A debate case torn apart by the opposition should not be used again until its faults have been eliminated and its weaknesses strengthened. Evidence, plainly inadequate, should be either discarded and replaced or supplemented with new material before the next debate. Faulty analysis can benefit from continued search on the vital issues. Consequently, research as well as the related activities go on without interruption until something like a perfect case is achieved, if such a case exists.

With some propositions, the perfect case could never be conceived even with continuous work because they deal with subject matter which constantly changes. The 1959 United States collegiate debate resolution contained such subject matter. The resolution, "Resolved: That the further development of nuclear weapons should be prohibited by international agreement," was debated during a period when nuclear weaponry was undergoing constant development and testing by many nations. Discoveries of significance were announced regularly throughout the debate season and debaters were obliged to alter their cases as regularly in order to keep up with the changes. With that proposition, debates often were won by the teams with evidence gleaned from the previous day's newspapers. Research, evidence gathering, analysis, case construction and alteration were never ending in that year. Normally, however, a good job of research early in the year should be sufficient for the rest of the year.

What we have just said about research may suggest that research is a difficult and time consuming process. While it is time consuming, research also can be interesting and enjoyable, and it is one of the most valuable skills a debater can learn. The research skills a debater acquires can be used in almost any other field of study and should be valuable tools in a career whatever that career may be.

Find References

The first step in research is to find out what references are available on the debate proposition. To find these references, consult general indexes for listings of books and articles that give an overview of the proposition. The following selected resources should be helpful in locating books and articles on the debate proposition: *Readers' Guide to Periodical Literature* — the major index in the area of general periodicals, this publication appears semi-monthly from September to June and monthly from June to September and probably is the most useful guide for debaters seeking references in American sources; *Social Science Index* and *Humanities Index* (previously called the *International Index to Periodical Literature*) — these indexes list references particularly in the social sciences and humanities found in scholarly journals and foreign publications; *New York Times Index* — published in bimonthly and annual editions, this index covers the content of each day's issues of the New York City newspaper, the *Times; Public Affairs Information Service Bulletin* — this weekly publication is a boon to debaters since it indexes about 1000 books, documents, and periodicals in political science, history, economics, social studies, and legislation; *The Times Index* —

published by the London Times, it is an index of the news printed in that newspaper; *Index to Legal Periodicals* — monthly publications in the legal field; and *Index Medicus* — monthly publications in medical journals.

After examining the general sources for reading references, consult next the more specialized resources for detailed and specialized data needed to support your arguments. The following specialized indexes or abstracts cover world-wide sources: *Education Index* — this index lists United States, Canadian, and other foreign periodicals, books, and pamphlets on educational subjects; *Historical Abstracts* — this digest presents abstracts of articles on world political, economic, and social history; *Sociological Abstracts* — this monthly publication summarizes important material in foreign and United States sociological publications; *Facts on File* — this weekly digest covers the important world news events; *Keesing's Contemporary Archives* — this London-published weekly deals with world economic and political news; *The Statesman's Yearbook* — this annual publication specializes in who's who in world political and economic geography; and *Psychological Abstracts* — a monthly publication summarizing important material published in psychological journals.

Prepare a Bibliography

A thorough examination of the available indexes and catalogues should reveal an abundance of books, periodicals, documents, articles, and other reference material on the subject matter of the debate proposition. In order to organize these sources for later reading, collect them into the form of a bibliography. A bibliography is a systematic compilation of references on a particular debate resolution or for that matter, on any other subject. Compiling a bibliography is the second step in research.

To assemble a bibliography, follow these instructions: (1) locate the pertinent references in the appropriate indexes and catalogues, (2) place each reference item on a separate file card, (3) record all of the information necessary to identify the publication, including, for books — author, title, place of publication, publisher, date of publication, and for periodicals — author, title of article, name of periodical, volume, number, date, page numbers of article, (4) place on each reference card any notes or comments about the reference, its author, its importance to your case, and (5) alphabetize these cards for convenience in use.

Read

The debater spends a majority of his research effort reading, and this reading has to pay off for him or he will be wasting his time and energy. So, our third concern in research, once the references have been located and bibliography constructed, is how to read the material in the bibliography.

Unfortunately the typical debate proposition covers a considerable amount of material and the amount may be more than the average debater can read before the debate season ends. Hence, some planning needs to be done before the reading begins. Rather than plod through the bibliography and read everything at once, it would be wiser to organize the reading. These suggestions may be helpful: (1) get the main idea, (2) determine the important details, (3) answer the stock issue questions, (4) evaluate, and (5) apply what you read.

Record Data

Problems come up while one reads on the debate proposition. One problem stems from the realization that it is almost impossible to determine what material may be useful and what may not until case construction begins. Another problem concerns material that may not be useful in case construction but could be beneficial in refutation. A similar problem relates to deciding what material should be saved because it may be useful later in the debate season. These problems affect what should be recorded.

Experience dictates that the debater should record everything he reads which is relevant to the proposition and passes the tests of evidence. Material will be available, consequently, whenever it may be needed.

Recording data constitutes the fourth step in debate research. How should a debater record data? Suggestions follow.

Most debaters record data gathered in their reading on file cards. These cards are sold in a variety of sizes, however, the cards 8 by 10 inches or 10 by 12 inches seem best suited for debaters' use. The cards, which are used rapidly as one reads and records, are stored in a file box, approximately the size of the cards and light-weight for easy handling.

Use a separate card for each distinct piece of information. These are arranged in a sequence appropriate to the affirmative and negative side as we explain in the next section. Championship debaters, it may be interesting to note, often accumulate thousands of file cards which they bring to each debate in large boxes.

What data should be placed on each card? The following biblio-graphical citations should be included: author's name, title of the publi-cation, name of periodical when appropriate, place of publication and name of publisher if a book, volume and number if a periodical, date of publication, and the page numbers. Also included on the card is the desired information selected from the reference as well as pertinent notes about the author.

What information should be recorded? Record that information which pertains to the issues of the debate, that is, the evidence needed to support the case and the evidence needed to refute possible cases of the opposition. Limit the amount of material placed on each card to a single item. Quote verbatim as much as possible although paraphrase lengthy material or highly abstract material. When you paraphrase, do so accurately. Do not misinterpret what the author says, intentionally or unintentionally.

What should be noted about the author? In parentheses at the bottom or on the back of the card, place a statement about the author's qualifi-cations. Learn about the author in one of several ways. Often his creden-tials are mentioned in the book or periodical; search the publication for comments about him. Occasionally you may have to check his qualifi-cations in a biographical reference volume like the *International Who's Who*.

Organize Data

The final step in debate research is to store the data gathered in a manner that will provide the fastest possible access to it. The average debater accumulates hundreds of file cards in a debate season. Begin-ners do not deal with hundreds of cards but handle at least fifty to a hundred. This number can prove troublesome, however, during a debate when they want a particular card to prove a particular argument and cannot find it without sorting through all of their cards. Organization of the cards, therefore, is important.

How should the cards be organized? No ideal method exists. The suggestions which follow however, may be helpful in establishing a system.

First, divide the cards according to the side, either affirmative or negative, on which they will be used. Some cards are useful on both the affirmative and negative sides. These should be duplicated, one for each side.

Second, divide the affirmative and negative cards into categories. The categories in the example below follow the stock issues and stock case outlines but other possible systems can be devised.

Affirmative

1. Definition of Terms
2. History of the Proposition
3. Problems of *Status Quo*
4. Causes of the Problems
5. Plans
6. Advantages of Plans
7. Miscellaneous

Negative

1. Definition of Terms
2. Attacks on Possible Affirmative Problems
3. Attacks on Possible Affirmative Plans
4. Benefits of *Status Quo*
5. Possible Repairs or Adjustments to *Status Quo*
6. Possible Alternative Plans
7. Miscellaneous

Each card in the categories should be coded for easy identification. For example, an affirmative card which defines a term could be coded "A-1," the "A" designates the affirmative side, "1" represents category one, definition of terms. A negative definition would be coded "N-1," the "N" represents the negative side while the "1" indicates the "definition of terms" category. Title each card and type or print the title and number of each card on a separate reference sheet so that you will find it quickly when you need the card in a debate.

The key to successful debate is preparation and the cornerstone in adequate preparation is research, the topic just covered. Five steps in the debate research process were described, including (1) finding references, (2) preparing a bibliography, (3) reading, (4) recording data, and (5) organizing data.

What we have said about these five steps necessarily ties in to what we said on proposition analysis — research and proposition analysis are allied activities and one compliments the other. To be able to analyze a proposition demands knowledge of it, and this knowledge comes from research on the proposition. Likewise, in order to be able to research the proposition, some idea of what to look for is necessary, and the guidelines imposed by proposition analysis serve that purpose. Proposition analysis relies on research and research requires proposition analysis. Read and analyze at the same time.

4

Argument: Evidence, Reasoning, and Claim

After the debater has collected the data, he faces the problem of selecting that data which will persuade the audience to accept his position on the proposition. To do this, he engages in constructing a series of arguments which he eventually will organize into an affirmative or a negative case.

For our purposes, an argument has three parts — claim, data and warrant. The *claim* is the conclusion the debater wants accepted. It is drawn from the *data* which has led the debater to make the conclusion. The debater must show the relationship which exists between the data and conclusion and he does this through the use of the *warrant*. Thus, claims are conclusions based on a consideration of data which are linked together by warrants.

The model of an argument is shown in Figure 1. Note that there are three basic elements to any argument — claim, data and warrant. The data leads the debater to make a claim through a warrant joining data and claim.

Figure 1. A Simple Argument in Debate

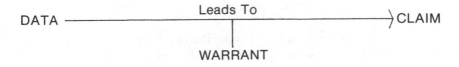

Figure 2 portrays a hypothetical argument for illustrative purposes using the Figure 1 model. Here the debater claims it will rain on July 28, 1980. He bases the claim on the data, the fact that it has rained on every July 28 for years. While the claim is based on the data, it is related to the data by the warrant which reasons "Rainfall in Honolulu follows an unvarying pattern." The warrant, in this case, could be stated or implied, and we expect it would be stated since most people do not know about Hawaii's rainfall.

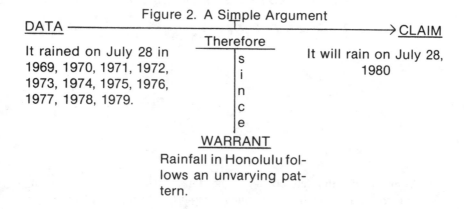

Figure 2. A Simple Argument

DATA ──────────────────────────────────→ CLAIM

Therefore

s
i
n
c
e

It rained on July 28 in 1969, 1970, 1971, 1972, 1973, 1974, 1975, 1976, 1977, 1978, 1979.

It will rain on July 28, 1980

WARRANT

Rainfall in Honolulu follows an unvarying pattern.

The two models represent simple arguments. Most arguments are much more complex, especially those in academic debate. Many include qualifiers, or reservations, or data for the warrants. We consider the complications in the following description of data, warrant and claim.

Data

Data is the material used to establish a claim. In its narrowest sense, it is the evidence used in academic debate, and, while debaters concern themselves primarily with evidence, in real-life or substantive debate, a broader conception of the term prevails.

In its larger sense, data consists of three types, labeled first-order, second-order, and third-order data. First-order data seems to be the most important in substantive debate because it is the only type upon which a meaningful argument can be developed. Third-order data usually is the least meaningful in substantive debate but the most valuable in academic debate, as we shall see.

First-order data is made up of intangible audience beliefs like opinion and knowledge. Anything the audience has an opinion on or has knowledge of can be used as data. However, finding out what a particular audience believes can be an extremely time-consuming undertaking.

Since first-order data constitutes the most persuasive form for the substantive debater, it is necessary for him to discover what his prospective audience believes. In preparing his persuasive message, therefore, the substantive debater must take into account the characteristics of his audience and engage in audience analysis of some sort.

However, the academic debater normally confronts a different type of audience, particularly in standard or cross-examination debate, than that of his substantive counterpart. The academic debater faces a group of judges who are evaluating his performance on the basis of what he says not on the basis of what they believe. In fact, judges are instructed to disregard their personal biases on the proposition and evaluate purely on what they hear. First-order data has little utilitarian value, therefore, in academic debate and we need not pursue the topic further.

Second-order data consists of asserted opinion and asserted information of the debater. When it is used, a secondary argument is introduced. The fault with second-order data, when used in academic debate, lies with the source of the data — the debater. Most debaters, since they are students enrolled in a variety of school activities, quite likely do not have the expertise on the subject matter of a debate proposition to converse about it as an expert could. And, second-order data calls for opinion or information from subject-matter experts. So, generally speaking, judges disregard the second-order data of academic debaters, and we do not recommend its use.

In practice, the data upon which most of an academic debater's arguments rest is *third-order data*. This type of data is referred to as "evidence," and its importance in academic debate causes us to devote a section below to it.

Supplementary arguments emerge with the use of third-order data in academic debate as they did with second-order data, and, like second-order data, the supplementary arguments of third-order data may be stated or implied. Figure 3 illustrates the emergence of two supplementary arguments, the first is stated, the second implied.

In Figure 3 the data in the main argument should be proved, otherwise it is merely first-order or second-order data, not acceptable in academic debate. Thus the data in the main argument becomes the claim in the first supplementary argument. Data and warrant are stated to support the claim. This raises a new question, did the Gallup Poll actually make this statement? Proof is needed, and the data of the first supplementary argument becomes the claim of the second. Again, data and warrant are provided, however, in an implied fashion. We take the debater's word, and the debater need not show the actual poll. Inci-

Figure 3. Third-Order Data with Supplementary Arguments

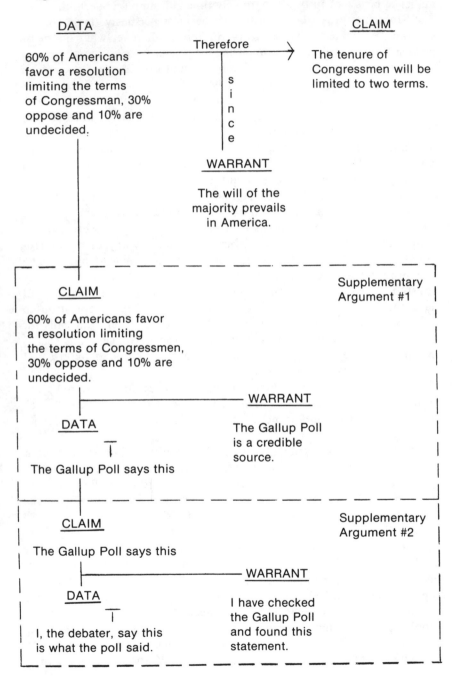

dentally, the Gallup Poll is generally believed to be a credible source. Unless the source is as well known as the Gallup Poll, the debater will have to demonstrate the source's credibility.

Evidence

Evidence is the factual statements originating with a source other than the debater, objects not created by the debater, and the opinions of persons other than the debater offered in support of the claims, or, conclusions, advanced by the debater. Four types appear, three of which debaters use almost exclusively.

Tangible Objects.

This type of evidence is most useful in substantive debate. Since tangible objects are real things capable of being touched, such as weapons, property deeds, fingerprint impressions, and photographs, evidence of this sort when used in the courtroom often determines the innocence or guilt of someone.

Although tangible objects are not ordinarily introduced as evidence in academic debate, the possibility always exists. A map or chart, for instance, may be useful in clarifying an argument, or a personal letter from an authority on the subject matter of a debate proposition may be useful datum to prove a claim.

Opinion.

An opinion is a statement based on one's own judgment rather than on certain knowledge. It is an interpretation of facts, or is a judgment of value concerning facts.

Opinions brought into a debate as evidence come from two sources, subject-matter authorities or laymen, that is, people who are non-experts. Opinions of authorities because of their expertise, normally are valued more highly than laymen, and constitute the better evidence. Opinions of laymen do not help the debater's case much unless they represent the opinions of vast numbers of people. Public opinion polls for instance, conducted by reputable agencies, have some merit and are useful if expert opinion is not available.

Factual Examples.

A fact is something that is known to be true, to exist or to happen, in the present or in the past. It is a living, growing, changing event with a ore that represents enough permanence so as to enable us to count on it. A factual example can be verified with reasonable assurance of accuracy because it actually happened, and, consequently, it constitutes the debater's strongest form of evidence.

Besides the factual example, there is another type of example, the hypothetical or fictional example. Often debaters create such examples for the purpose of clarifying or making a point more meaningful. They are useless as evidence, however.

Statistics.

Statistics are factual examples grouped together and reported in numerical form. When used to support claims, they are usually formulated in terms of the number of cases, percentage of cases, or rate of frequency of cases, such as, "Now consider the significance of 9,000 men. It is one-sixtieth of the Nationalist Chinese army. It is one-two-hundred-and-seventieth of the Red Chinese army. It is 4/100 of 1% of the American army."

Since they refer to a large number of instances of a similar nature, statistics are valuable as proof. They are difficult to communicate, however, and some suggestions are in order for their use: round the figures (instead of 9,127 men, round the figure to 9,000), don't use statistics too much, relate them closely to the argument by showing their impact on it, and summarize their meaning.

Tests of Evidence.

Any time evidence is used to support a claim, the evidence should be tested. It should fit the argument under consideration. It should be complete. Its originator should be competent to report the evidence. And, all conflicting evidence should be accounted for. Three tests can be applied to all types of evidence in order to determine their adequacy. These are the tests of relevancy, source competency, and validity. We will consider the tests in detail when we describe the twin processes of refutation and rebuttal.

Warrants

Another part of an argument is the relationship which links the evidence with the debater's conclusion or claim. This relationship we will refer to as a "warrant" or the link holding the two other parts together.

The warrant is the statement that shows the reasoning the debater must have gone through in order to link the data to the claim. It also may show the assumptions on which the claim is based or the method by which the evidence was evaluated. It is a "because," a "why," or a "since" kind of statement.

There are three types — motivational, authoritative, and substantive. *Motivational warrants* are based on assumptions concerning why persons act as they do in certain situations. We do things because we want to, because by doing so we satisfy our desires, because the things we do represent something we value, or because the things we do appeal to one or several of our emotions such as joy, fear, love, happiness, anger, and so forth. Hence, things are seen to be good or bad, beneficial or harmful, because they are seen as satisfying or not satisfying our desires or fulfilling some other emotional-based factor. For the debater, motivational warrants present a challenge — what is seen as good by one listener may be considered bad by another. The debater, therefore, must find the motivational warrants which will be accepted by a particular audience.

Authoritative warrants relate to the credibility of the source of the debater's evidence. The more credible the debater's sources are in the listener's mind, the more credible will be what the source says.

Substantive warrants are based on assumptions that refer to relationships among events in the external world — events which are interdependent, and connected in a systematic, regular, permanent and predictable fashion. The relationships of this sort are so frequently employed in debate that the six types justify examination.

1. *Causation.* Causation suggests that one thing causes another. Good teachers produce good debaters. Hard work and intelligence produce knowledgeable students. Smoking chimneys cause air pollution. Causation can proceed either from cause to effect, that is, from producer to produced, as in the three examples just mentioned, or from effect to cause, produced to producer, as in "air pollution is caused by smoking chimneys" and "good debaters result from good teachers."

2. *Sign.* Sign relationship, closely akin to causation, hence, often debaters confuse the two, assumes that two or more things exist together. Thus, when we reason from sign, we argue that because two things are so close, the presence or absence of one may be taken as an indication of the presence or absence of the other. If we see a man running to catch a train, it is a sign that he is late. If we saw people wearing heavy coats with hats on their heads, it is a sign that it is cold outside. However, the debater should exercise caution when using or hearing a sign warrant. A good many are fallacious, including most of the superstitions some people believe in.

3. *Analogy.* Whenever we argue on the basis of the substantive warrant known as analogy, we draw a conclusion or state a claim about some data from its similarity to other data. Through a comparison of the similarity, we reason if two situations or elements are alike in known respects, then they must be alike in other, unknown respects.

4. *Generalization and Classification.* These two substantive warrant types are virtually the opposite of each other, hence, we will discuss them together. Generalization (commonly called the inductive thought-pattern) assumes that what is true of a sample from a class is also true of the other members of that class, in other words, reasoning from the particular to the general. Classification (the deductive thought-pattern) assumes that what is true of the class is also true of the individual members of that class, that is, reasoning from the general to the particular.

Of the two, generalization is most commonly used by debaters. When it is used, it is characterized by a limited amount of data, by an implied warrant that the data typifies the class to which they belong, and by a claim that most, or all of the others, in the class have the same qualities.

Classification warrants are characterized by data that asserts a particular thing is a member of a class, by a warrant which assumes that a certain quality is typical of the class, and by a claim that concludes the particular thing referred to in the data has the quality typical of the class.

Tests of Warrants.

There are appropriate tests to measure the probability of warrants and the tests of substantive warrants are especially useful to debaters. They need to be described, and we do so when we examine refutation.

Claims

The third part of an argument is the claim, the explicit belief produced by the data and warrant, which the debater wants his audience to accept. The four types of claims roughly correspond to the four types of issues over which people tend to argue. Phrased as questions, these four types of issues are: "Is it?" "What is it?" "What is its quality?" "What should be done about it?" An argument designed to answer one of these issue-questions logically concludes with a claim. Each issue leads to a different claim, therefore, four claims, one for each issue, are identifiable. These are designative, definitive, evaluative, and advocative.

Designative claims relate to the issue, "Is it?", and as such they deal with fact — is, was, or will something be so? *Definitive claims* answer the question, "What is it?", and as such are concerned with definitions. *Evaluative claims* answer the what-is-its-quality question, and deal with values, or the relative merit of an idea, object, or action. *Advocative claims* answer the what-should-be-done-about-it question, and concern the making of policy. Most academic debate propositions are advocative claims, since the debate proposition advocates that the present system should be replaced with the new system suggested by the proposition.

To conclude, an argument consists of three parts — data or evidence, warrant or the reasoning involved in the argument, and claim or the conclusion the debater draws. Not all arguments are perfect. In fact, few are. Their imperfections should be revealed when certain tests are applied to them. The imperfections constitute material for refutation and we will describe how to locate the imperfections when we consider refutation. Before doing so, it is necessary to find out how to integrate arguments into a case, either an affirmative or a negative case.

5

The Affirmative Case

The affirmative case forms the structural basis of the debate. It stakes out the ground for argument. Unless the affirmative approach to the proposition is unorthodox, the negative must accept the definitions and philosophy of the affirmative, and argue on those terms. The affirmative case, therefore, must be well-organized and defendable.

Clear organization is vital for two reasons: (1) so that the affirmative position is clear and can be easily followed, and (2) so that the issues have force as well as clarity and, therefore, must be the areas of controversy. A well-organized affirmative helps insure a clear debate. A messy, rambling affirmative case usually makes a debate confusing and sloppy, even against a good negative team, for the negative takes most of its organization from the affirmative.

The need to have a defendable case is obvious. The negative team has to destroy the affirmative case, hence, the negative debaters will be looking for weaknesses in the affirmative case. The affirmative must try to eliminate the weaknesses in constructing their case and be prepared to rebuild any weaknesses discovered by the negative during the debate.

Case Requirements

The affirmative case must be much more than well-organized and defendable. The case must fulfill the requirements of propositionality, presumption, the burden of proof, significance, and inherency.

Propositionality.

In debate, the affirmative is required to uphold the proposition and debate the subject matter it represents. To do so, the affirmative has to deal with topicality, extra-topicality, and justification. These three issues relate to the "propositionality" requirement of the affirmative case.

Topicality raises the question: "Does the affirmative case meet the demands of the debate proposition?" An affirmative team debating the proposition, "Resolved: that a comprehensive program of penal reform should be adopted throughout the United States," should offer as part of its plan a comprehensive program on penal reform which would be adopted throughout the United States in order to be topical. Anything less would not fulfill the topicality issue. However, anything more or anything irrelevant to the topic raises the extra-topicality issue. Conceiving a penal reform program for the whole world would exceed the bounds of the proposition and would be extra-topical. On the other hand, conceiving a comprehensive program of social reform would be irrelevant to the proposition and, again, extra-topical. In addition, whatever the affirmative offers must be justifiable. That is, the reasons for making the change must be important enough to warrant the change.

Presumption.

Presumption means that conditions as they now exist are all right until proven otherwise. In other words, a person is innocent until he is proven guilty. The negative has presumption in its favor and the affirmative must overcome the presumption if its case is to be considered sound. Thus, the affirmative has to present a case which contains good and sufficient reasons for changing from the present or for altering existing conditions.

Burden of Proof.

The affirmative is obligated to prove that existing conditions are faulty and a change is needed. Hence, the affirmative case must include sufficient evidence to support whatever claims are made that the present is faulty.

Significance.

That which is proved by the affirmative must be significant, that is, the faults, whatever they may be, must be major ones, ones that merit correcting or eliminating. They must be significant in both a quantitative and a qualitative sense. The quantity must be large enough to be worthy of debate; the value of the quantity must also be worthy of debate. For example, the death of a million ants in California because of a drought would not be significant to the average person. Certainly the quantity is large enough, but few people value ants enough to do much about supplying California's ants with water. Qualitatively, significance is absent in the ant example, although quantitatively the number is high.

Inherency.

One of the stock issues concerns inherency — the "why" of a problem's existence. The "why" is treated at several levels, two of which bear repeating. These are the causal and remedial levels. The causal level concerns the causes of the problem. "What caused the problem?" we ask. To answer the question, we need to find the root causes. The remedial level relates to past efforts to solve the problem. "What has been done to alleviate the causes, if anything?" we ask. The answer comes when we uncover what has been done and why whatever was done did not succeed. If it had succeeded, there would be no reason to debate the resolution.

Also, inherency presents at least two barriers — structural and attitudinal. Structurally, an affirmative plan may not be able to be implemented because of some structural force, a legal mandate, for instance. Should a law say that the affirmative can't do what it wants to do, then it can't be done regardless of how hard the affirmative desires that it be done.

The "attitudinal" barrier stems from an attitude which would prevent the implementation of the affirmative's solution. Today the federal government prohibits the use of fireworks under certain circumstances. In Honolulu, the majority of the people hold a favorable attitude toward fireworks' shooting and shoot them regularly. The police do not interfere much because they would have to arrest thousands of people to stop the practice. The barrier is the attitude of the people. Because the government's plan of prohibiting fireworks' shooting failed to take into account that barrier, the plan, in Honolulu at least, is a failure.

Case Structures

At one time there were only two basic affirmative case structures in use, the traditional need-plan-advantages case and the newer comparative advantages case which gained popularity in the 1960's. Today there is a wide variety of affirmative case structures being debated, and, although a team may only use one or two in the debate season, the debaters should be familiar with the others so that they will be able to refute them if they hear them when they are on the negative.

We will describe seven affirmative case possibilities: (1) need-plan-advantages, (2) comparative advantages, (3) goals-criteria, (4) alternative-justification, (5) effects-oriented, (6) on-balance, and (7) comparative need.

Need-Plan-Advantages.

The need-plan-advantages structure revolves around a problem and a solution to correct the problem. The affirmative must demonstrate that an inherent problem exists in the *status quo* and that this problem needs to be changed. As they do so, the affirmative team must indicate the causes of the problem, must propose a plan to correct the problem by removing the causes, and, finally, must demonstrate how the plan eliminates the causes.

That strategy involves an analysis based on the five stock issues: Is there a need for a change? Is the need inherent? Will the plan meet the need? Is the plan practical? Do the advantages of the plan outweigh the disadvantages?

In developing the need for a change, inherent flaws must be presented in order to persuade an audience to alter its currently held belief. These inherent flaws, or needs for a change, can be structured in the following manner:

I. There is a need for a change because

    A. A serious problem is present in the *status quo*

        1. Example of the problem
        2. Example of the problem
        3. Example of the problem

  B. This problem is caused by certain inherent characteristics of the present system

    1. Characteristic 1 causes this problem

      a. Evidence
      b. Evidence

    2. Characteristic 2 causes this problem

      a. Evidence
      b. Evidence

    3. Characteristic 3 causes this problem

      a. Evidence
      b. Evidence

(Repeat this structure for each additional need.)

The affirmative not only justifies the change in the *status quo* but also shows that the change should be related to the specific plan advocated by the affirmative.

The number of details in the plan depends upon the proposition being debated. Whatever the number, the plan should be described as specifically, concisely, and clearly as possible. It should be organized into no more than three or four main categories. For example, the categories of structure, function, method of enforcement, and finance which could be organized in this way:

  II. The affirmative proposes the following plan to solve the problems cited in the *status quo*:

    A. Its structure will consist of . . .

    B. It will function in the following manner . . .

    C. Its method of enforcement will be . . .

    D. Its means of financing will be . . .

At this point, the strategy shifts from describing what has happened to predicting what could happen if the plan is carried out. The analysis for stock issues, 3, 4, and 5 should be applied in developing prediction, and evidence is necessary to support such prediction. Note how the two are handled in the following outline of the "advantages" part of the traditional strategy:

III. Many advantages will result from the affirmative plan

    A. The plan will remove the problems and their causes cited in the *status quo*

        1. Problem 1 is corrected

            a. Evidence
            b. Evidence

        2. Problem 2 is corrected

            a. Evidence
            b. Evidence

(Repeat for all problems.)

    B. The plan is practical for it can be implemented

        1. Evidence
        2. Evidence

    C. The plan will have additional advantages

        1. It will have advantage 1

            a. Evidence
            b. Evidence

        2. It will have advantage 2

            a. Evidence
            b. Evidence

(Repeat for additional advantages.)

Comparative Advantages.

A product of the 1960's, the comparative advantages case caught a tide of change prevalent at the time and rode the crest of popularity to the present. Limited in application, the case is usually misused by neophyte coaches and debaters, by those desiring a ride on the bandwagon, or by those seeking a competitive advantage. The case is properly used when real, inherent and significantly damaging evils do not seem to exist in the present system. Since there is no compelling harm, a debate using this structure revolves around two policies: (1) the present as normally upheld by the negative, and (2) the new, supposedly more advantageous policy or plan advocated by the affirmative.

Because this case compares a new policy with the old, the plan is presented first, since it isn't possible to compare the two policies until the proposed policy is known. Following the plan, the plan's advantages are given. These provide a rationale for making the change. The advantages must be both "significant" and "inherent" to the proposition. They must be significant in the sense that they are more important, more momentous, and more superior than the advantages of the *status quo*. They must be inherent in that they are unique to the plan, which is to say, the advantages can only be achieved by adopting the plan.

The following outline suggests a way to structure the comparative advantages case, frequently presented entirely by the first affirmative constructive speaker:

I. Introduction and statement of the proposition.

II. Definition of terms.

III. The plan.

IV. The plan's advantages.

V. Comparison of the advantages with the conditions of the *status quo.*

VI. Demonstration of significance and inherency of the advantages.

VII. Summary.

Goals-Criteria.

A number of affirmative cases of varying sophistication have appeared under labels such as "criteria," "rationale," and "goal." All seem to be similar enough to lump together under the goals-criteria heading, and the case described here represents such an amalgamation.

A goals-criteria case is an affirmative case which features goals built on value judgments. The goals act as the criteria by which the acceptability of the proposal is judged. In this type of case, the affirmative sets forth goals which are either goals of the *status quo* but not operating in the present sytem or which are not present in the *status quo* and should be. The plan advocated by the affirmative provides the means to implement these goals — goals which supposedly will produce benefits to the society.

The goals dealt with can be broadly based in postulated fundamental tenets or values of society (*e.g.*, recognition of life's sanctity, keeping the world safe for democracy, and maintaining national security) or the goals can be more limited by being oriented to the values found in the subject matter of the debate proposition. In either case, the goals are chosen because they are deemed desirable bases upon which a policy is formulated.

The goals advocated by the affirmative may be *status quo* goals which were not attained or new goals, that is, ones not sought by the *status quo*. Thus the major emphasis in this case switches, depending on whether the affirmative recognizes present goals or presents new ones. Should the affirmative accept the present goals, then the approach is to demonstrate why the goals are not being met and what can be done to meet them. Should the affirmative reject present goals, then the affirmative offers new goals and argues for them.

In developing the goals-criteria case, we advocate the use of the following organizational pattern:

I.   Present a philosophy or observation of the case.

II.   Establish the goal or goals that should be attained.

    A.   Demonstrate that the goal is worth attaining.

III.   State the resolution formally.

IV.   Define the terms of the resolution.

V.   Present the affirmative plan.

VI.   First major contention.

    A.   Establish the significance of the harm when the goal is unfulfilled by the *status quo*.

    B.   Present the inherent reason the *status quo* is precluded from attaining the goal.

    C.   Establish how the new proposal better meets or attains the goal than the *status quo*.

VII.   Second major contention (optional — used to support second goal).

    A.   Use the same pattern established under part VI.

VIII. Summarize debate.

IX.   Present closing statement.

The goals-criteria case provides a more effective and substantial approach for debating the goals underlying policy actions and the values those goals support. This case is valuable in that it (1) provides an opportunity to determine the *prima facie* requirements for a proposition of value, (2) forces debaters to analyze substantively, to attack, and to defend values as a structural part of affirmative analysis, and (3) more realistically features the significance of the value itself as a part of policy formulation.

Alternative-Justification.

Allegedly introduced by Harvard University debaters in 1972, the alternative-justification case offers in a single debate, two or more parallel affirmative plans, each of which is a legitimate, if narrow, interpretation of the debate resolution. While the comparative advantages case defends one policy for several independent reasons, the alternative-justification case upholds several independent policies, each with its own advantages. Supposedly the comparative advantages case can win by successfully defending any one of its advantages, then the alternative-justification case also can win by successfully defending any one of its plans. The case, therefore, advances several sets of plan-advantage relationships, each of which is independent of the others and each a legitimate interpretation of and a justification for the resolution.

The structure of this case perhaps is more clearly understood with an example. Using the resolution, "Resolved: that the federal government should establish a system of compulsory wage and price controls," the sample case is outlined as follows:

I.   The resolution will guard against the ravages of inflation. Plan setting a percentage ceiling on all wage and price increases.

    A. Inflation generates harmful distortions in the economic system.

    B. Current efforts are incapable of halting inflation.

    C. Strict controls can effectively halt inflation.

II.   The resolution will protect the poor from economic discrimination. Plan outlawing excessively high food prices in ghetto areas and establishing higher minimum wages.

    A. Unreasonably low wages and high prices afflict the American poor.

    B. No mechanism exists to curb this ghetto-gouging.

    C. Federal controls can stop ghetto-gouging.

III.   The resolution will minimize the suffering of the chronically ill. Plan lowering the prices of patent medicines and regulating pharmacists' wages.

    A. Millions of chronically ill cannot afford necessary prescription drugs.

    B.   Present controls on prescription costs are ineffective.

    C.   Federal wage and price standards will guarantee lower prescription costs.

In the example, three plans are presented, each a justifiable alternative to the *status quo*. Each, of course, must satisfy the burden of proof and fulfill the requirements of significance and inherency demanded in any of the other affirmative approaches. Note that the example reveals a principal fault of the alternative-justification case. The fault is too many issues introduced into the debate, and a possible reduction could result in the quality of analysis.

The case is faulted for other reasons, one of which is the reasoning behind the case. The logic seems to suggest: "it doesn't make much difference if the judge accepts all the plans but by accepting at least one, the affirmative wins." Thus, advocating a new policy isn't the goal; winning the debate is.

Effects-Oriented.

An occasional proposition involves a problem the basic cause of which is impossible or undesirable to eliminate. Then the effects-oriented case has great utilitarian value. This case treats the harms of the present system without removing the inherent causes of the harms. The crucial aspect of this case is the plan. The affirmative conceives a plan that is capable of operating within the framework of the present system, yet is different in principle from the present. The plan alleviates the harms of the present while allowing their causes to remain.

The rationale of the case may be better understood through a simple illustration. Joe drives a truck for a delivery company. Efficient, polite and personable, he represents the company well and is a definite asset dealing with customers. However, he gets into a lot of accidents and bangs up the truck he drives. Apparently a cultural belief of his is the cause of the accidents. His culture does not attach much significance to material things and as a consequence he treats such things with indifference. Realizing Joe's value as a company contact with customers, the company solved the accident problem by hiring a driver to assist Joe in deliveries. The company, thus, alleviated the harms of the present system, the truck damage, but not the cause, Joe's attitude toward material things. The effects-oriented case operates in that fashion.

A proposition concerned with a problem caused by a deep-seated attitude, as in Joe's case, would ideally fit the effects-oriented case. Cases built on so-called *attitudinal inherency* arguments could utilize the effects-oriented approach. Such arguments identify an unchanging attitude as the cause. The attitude is allegedly inherent and it cannot be removed, therefore, it must be circumvented.

On-Balance.

This case is developed either according to the need-plan-benefits approach or the comparative advantages approach, depending upon the proposition debated. Basically, the on-balance case argues that the high costs of the present policy do not offset the few benefits realized from it. But the proposition offers a policy not as costly with more benefits — the costs are on-balance, so to speak. The need-plan-benefits structure fits this approach when there is an obvious, inherent cause responsible for the high costs. The comparative advantages structure, on the other hand, works when there is no identifiably inherent cause for the costs.

Useful for those propositions where the affirmative should maximize the costs, the cost issue is developed by demonstrating that the *status quo* is either ineffective or unnecessary. The alleged benefits can be obtained in other ways, yet the cost of abandoning the present policy in favor of the new one will be nil. For example, some foreign policy experts contend that the U.S.A. should not intervene militarily in other country's internal affairs. The costs are too high in lost lives, supplies, and loss of prestige, while the gains are few, if any at all. The few benefits, if any, could have been achieved without military intervention, and the lives, supplies, and possible loss of prestige from military failure could have been saved.

Comparative-Need.

The close of the 1960's saw the advent of comparative-need cases. Useful for propositions with a less than all-pervading evil, the case bears a resemblance to the comparative advantages approach, and, in fact, it may be an appropriate alternative to the comparative advantages when there is a comparatively potential harm.

When using this case, the affirmative reasons in one of two ways. First, it recognizes that a degree of harm exists in the *status quo*. Although that harm is not so great as to cause immediate disastrous effects, it nevertheless exists and will continue to do so, or it may even become a "significant" harm, unless the *status quo* is changed. Second, the affirmative recognizes that a harm could occur in the future unless the *status quo* is changed now.

In developing the case, the affirmative first sets forth an observation or two about the *status quo* on which their case will hinge. For example an affirmative using the comparative-need case with the proposition, "Resolved: that the Federal Government should adopt a comprehensive program to control land use in the United States," would find a comparative need in energy production. Then it could advance the observation, "the United States has an increased need for energy." After proving the accuracy of the observation, the affirmative, in its second stage of analysis, would contend that, compared to the present system, a harm exists and it stems from the *status quo*. To use the energy example, the affirmative could show that the United States has such an abundant coal supply that it could take care of all the nation's energy needs for the next hundred years. Should coal fields be developed, then a harm in the *status quo* would be eliminated. The harm would be the inflationary balance of trade deficit — a deficit which comes from dependence on foreign oil. While "high" now, but acceptable because of the demand, the deficit could become disastrous if allowed to continue. This harm, although less than all-pervading, does exist and it stems from present land-use policies. To conclude its case, the affirmative shows that the comparative harm would be removed by the adoption of the affirmative resolution. Then, it presents its plan and the advantages that will handle the harm.

The case revolves around what appears to be a potential harm, or harms, comparatively speaking, to the *status quo*. The harm, even though only a potential one, nonetheless, should be dealt with. It can be dealt with through the resolution's adoption.

Speaker Duties

Each affirmative speaker has certain general responsibilities to meet or duties to perform. Likewise, each speech must accomplish certain general purposes. These are outlined below for each affirmative speech in the order of their presentation. Recognize that the seven affirmative case structures just described impose specific requirements of their own. Debaters will have to adapt the general duties stated next to the requirements of whatever case they utilize.

First Affirmative Constructive Speech.

Purpose: To introduce the debate proposition, to present as much of the affirmative case as possible in an attempt to establish a *prima facie* case.

Duties: These minimal duties are completed in the typical first affirmative — (1) a greeting or salutation followed by a statement of the proposition; for example, "We're happy to be here today to debate this important resolution, 'Resolved: That . . .' "; (2) definition of the terms used in the resolution; (3) an outline of the entire affirmative case; (4) the presentation and development of the issues; (5) a brief explanation of the plan and advantages; (6) a summary.

Remarks: This speech is the only one in the debate that may be prepared in advance; as such, it should be carefully developed, worded, rehearsed, and fluently delivered.

Second Affirmative Constructive Speech.

Purpose: To answer the major negative attacks and to present the remainder of the affirmative case.

Duties: (1) a salutation; (2) a reply to negative questions about the definitions of terms; (3) rebuttal of the issues presented by the first affirmative in view of the negative refutation; (4) the presentation of the affirmative plan, if not given by the first affirmative, and proof that the plan solves the problem demonstrated by the issues; (5) refutation of negative case, if presented; and (6) a brief summary of the entire affirmative case — resolution, definitions, needs, plan, advantages.

Remarks: The second affirmative speech differs greatly from the first, in that it is organized and prepared spontaneously in response to the objections of the negative speaker. In addition, the speaker may have many negative objections to deal with and these could take all of his time. If they do, this affirmative speaker should either deal with the most vital objections or blend them all into a few manageable points.

First Affirmative Rebuttal Speech.

Purpose: To rebuild the affirmative case after fifteen minutes of negative attack.

Duties: (1) restate the entire affirmative case by (a) taking each issue in order and quickly rebuilding it with proper evidence, (b) rebuilding the plan, and (c) showing the plan's advantages; and (2) a summary.

Remarks: The affirmative must regain control of the debate in this speech and consequently shift the burden of rebuttal back to the negative. If the speaker does his job well, the negative should end up on the defensive again.

Second Affirmative Rebuttal Speech.

Purpose: To answer the remaining issues and summarize the entire debate for the affirmative.

Duties: This speaker, like the previous one, should review the debate from his side's point of view but he should also rebuild any points successfully refuted by the negative. His duties, therefore, may proceed in this fashion: (1) refute any key arguments of the negative, (2) review the affirmative case for the last time, and (3) conclude the debate.

Remarks: As in the case of the final negative speaker, the final affirmative should emphasize negative weaknesses and affirmative strengths, and should create the impression that the resolution should be adapted.

6

The Negative Case

The major difference between the negative and the affirmative case is that although the affirmative has the burden of *proof,* the negative has the burden of *rejoinder.* In other words, while the affirmative prepares for the defense of its particular approach against all possible attacks, the negative must prepare various attacks against a variety of possible affirmative cases. Therefore, the negative team must be flexible and thoroughly prepared. Because of the need for flexibility, we cannot suggest rigid formats for the negative constructive speeches as we did for the affirmative.

Yet, we can suggest certain principles for the negative speeches and ways to counter the affirmative.

Principles of Negative Debating

Four principles are worth the negative team's attention. These concern presumption, proof, affirmative jargon, and negative psychology.

Presumption.

The negative has presumption in its favor, and often we overlook this principle. When it defends the *status quo,* the negative is not arguing that the present system is perfection incarnate. The negative does not need to prove "no" to the debate resolution; it only has to prove "not yes." That is to say, the resolution must withstand rigorous testing to demonstrate that it is significant beyond a reasonable doubt. Just as a prosecutor must demonstrate guilt "beyond a reasonable doubt," so, too, must the affirmative prove the proposed change would be significantly better.

Proof.

The second principle concerns the quantity and quality of the affirmative's proof. The negative must clearly understand just because the affirmative says it is so, that doesn't make it is so. The affirmative, in other words, has to prove its case, and the case must pass the tests of evidence and reasoning. Should the case fail to do so, the negative has them. Further, the negative must recognize that the affirmative's case, whatever it may be, is a hypothetical one. The affirmative cannot prove that the change they advocate will lead to the benefits they claim. The affirmative can only hypothesize that the benefits will occur. On the other hand, the negative deals with facts. Negative debaters know what the *status quo* has done and what it is capable of doing, and they should take full advantage of the demonstrable truth of their position, exploiting the necessarily tentative nature of the affirmative's position.

Jargon.

An occasional affirmative team will hide a weak case or cover up a weak point by resorting to debate jargon. For instance, challenged by the negative, the affirmative replies, "Ours is a goals-criteria case. We're dealing with goals postulated in the fundamental tenets of the American society. We've shown that these goals are necessary and we've met the requirements of the case." Nonverbally, they are saying, "My, you negative debaters are stupid. You don't know what goals-criteria means!" By using the jargon, they are trying to shift the negative's attention away from the weaknesses. Weak points exist in any case regardless of its name, and the negative should be aware of this. Rather than to be confused by the jargon attached to affirmative cases, the negative should look for the holes in the case. Given the limitations of debater ingenuity, the weaknesses are there and the negative needs to find them.

Negative Team Psychology.

Negative debaters should maintain a certain psychological attitude as they debate. The main component of this attitude is the quality of aggressiveness, but it is never flavored with sarcasm or ridicule. Rather, it is tempered with the impression of sincere and earnest conviction that the affirmative proposals are completely unsound. This aggressive attitude must be maintained at all times. The second constructive speaker, especially, must not let the fact that his partner is about to follow him in the rebuttals lull him into apathetic debating. The good negative team never lets up. It is constantly on the attack, always attempting to place the affirmative team on the defensive. If the affirmative team can ever get on the "offense," the negative team will probably lose, due to the affirmative's final words in the last rebuttal.

Finally, a caution is in order to negative debaters: don't be sarcastic. You may be tempted at times, especially if the technique has been used against you. Furthermore, don't merely quibble on minor points. True, an aggressive debater keeps the floor full of a large number of objections. Even more important than quantity is the quality of your arguments. If you find a weakness in a particular opposing argument, concentrate upon it and force the issue. But don't waste a great deal of time, for example, in asking innumerable questions, or absurdly objecting to definitions which are fairly orthodox. Remember, however, that you must contest tricky definitions, for they usually form the basis of an unorthodox case. Recall also that most definition-squabble debates are messy and not satisfying. If you must contest definitions, do so, of course, then attempt to meet the affirmative on its own terms as well.

Case Structures

With seven affirmative case structures to prepare for, negative-side debaters can no longer rely entirely on the strategies of the 1960's, those of repairs, pure refutation, and the counterplan. They have to broaden their negative-case repertoire to include ways of defeating each of the seven affirmatives. In the following explanation of negative structures, we discuss the ways of handling each affirmative case and, in doing so, we attach the affirmative case label to the negative structure.

Need-Plan-Advantages.

The negative has five possible ways to counter the need-plan-advantages affirmative. These are the direct refutation, *status quo,* repairs, counterplan and problems structures.

1. *Direct Refutation* ("Deny Everything"). The first type of negative approach is perhaps the simplest, and yet the most complex of the five. In the *direct refutation* approach, the debaters have no set case

prepared in advance, but attempt to defeat any and all affirmative cases without advancing constructive contentions of their own. Of course, to a large extent, all five of the negative approaches are based upon direct attack, but this is the only approach based entirely on it. The direct refutation approach is the easiest of the five, then, in that nothing must be prepared in advance. It is the most difficult in that nothing is set up in advance. The negative team relies entirely upon its ability to defeat an affirmative case with arguments which they can advance against the case spontaneously.

2. *Status Quo.* The term *status quo* (synonymous with "present situation" or "existing conditions") is also the label for a type of negative approach. It means that the negative defends completely the existing situation, and objects to any change from it. In addition to direct attack on the affirmative, the negative team, using the *status quo* approach, prepares in advance specific reasons why existing conditions should be maintained. Therefore, the *status quo* approach overcomes a major objection we raised to the *direct refutation* approach: arguments are prepared in advance. However, the *status quo* approach poses a disadvantage. Usually most existing conditions are not perfect (especially controversial issues delineated by national debate topics), therefore, the *status quo* is often difficult to sell. When a debater does not have complete confidence in the *status quo,* he should not choose this negative approach.

3. *Repairs* (Modified *Status Quo*). The third approach to the negative overcomes the disadvantages of the *status quo* approach. In the "repairs" case, the negative defends the basic structure of the *status quo,* but readily concedes that the framework should be "repaired" or modified. However, the negative must *not* advocate drastic structural changes, or the case is not *repairs,* but *counterplan,* which we will discuss next. Admittedly, where the line is drawn between a "structural" and "nonstructural" change from the *status quo* is a moot point, but the negative must make an attempt in this direction. Assuming that the negative has made a justifiable distinction and has, in fact, a "repairs" argument, the team has a disadvantage. They are conceding, not conceding much, but conceding. And anytime anything is conceded in a debate, the opponents will make much of it. Usually, the "repairs" approach is used in conjunction with a basic "minimization" attack upon the affirmative need contentions. In other words, the negative cannot defeat the needs, but the team can make them look quite small. The negative contends that the affirmative has exaggerated their importance. Conceding a minimal need, however, the negative argues that a few minimal nonstructural changes in the *status quo* will repair it nicely, and the "drastic" affirmative plan is unnecessary. When the "repairs" case is

handled correctly, it's a pesky negative approach, and one of the most common ones used.

4. *Counterplan*. The fourth possible negative approach to a need-plan-advantages affirmative is called the counterplan. When it uses a counterplan, the negative team fully concedes the need (often it adds other similar "needs" which the affirmative has failed to develop), then suggests a different solution. Therefore, the entire debate revolves around the question: "Which solution is best?" The negative, then, must prove that its counter-solution is better than the affirmative plan. This somewhat unorthodox approach is dangerous, and we do not recommend that it be used. Here are four of the pitfalls:

1. Many judges consider it tricky and somewhat unethical.

2. This is the only negative approach where the negative assumes part of the burden of proof — something the negative does not want, especially when they're listening to the final affirmative rebuttal. In a counterplan situation, the negative and the affirmative split the burden of proof. The question is not "Will the affirmative plan work?" but "Which plan is better?"

3. The negative plan must come from outside the area staked out for the affirmative to defend, yet it must still answer any conceivable affirmative need contentions. This is difficult, but a "must," for if the affirmative can adopt the negative proposal, they may add it to theirs, and the negative loses by default.

4. Finally, the negative concedes a tremendous amount of the affirmative case, even though it gains the advantages of a surprise attack, and even though the concession is logical with a counterplan.

5. *The Problem Case*. The problem case, the final type of negative attack on the affirmative need-plan-advantages case, is often useful when the negative team does not choose to repair or defend the *status quo,* but still wishes to make constructive contentions. The problems approach, then, most closely resembles the "direct refutation" approach which we discussed first. But it is direct refutation without complete reliance upon the impromptu construction of arguments. This approach, like the others, begins with a specific attack on the affirmative case. In addition to this attack, however, the debaters discuss inherent "problems" which the affirmative must consider in light of their stand upon the resolution. Obviously, "problems" will vary, depending upon the affirmative inter-

pretation of the resolution. So the negative team using this approach must prepare at least ten or twelve different problems of from two to three minutes in length each, and select the ones it will use after it hears the affirmative case in the debate. Usually from two to four are used in each round. If the affirmative case is extremely unorthodox and none of the problems fit, then the team shifts to a direct-refutation approach. With good problem construction, however, a shift is rarely necessary. Thus, the problems case overcomes most of the disadvantages of the direct refutation approach, while maintaining the basic advantages of complete flexibility. For experienced debaters, we recommend it highly.

Comparative Advantages.

Unlike the need-plan-advantages case, in a comparative advantages case, the affirmative does not argue that a significant harm is caused by the *status quo*. Instead, the affirmative proposes an entirely new plan, then seeks to prove that advantages will accrue from the new plan which would not result from the *status quo*. The key difference between this case and the need-plan-advantages case is that the comparative advantages case does not argue harms. Rather, it argues plan advantages. It argues that the proposed plan is advantageous when compared to the *status quo*. The reason for making the change stems from the benefits the new proposal will bring. The need-plan-advantages case is concerned with correcting detrimental defects in the *status quo*.

The comparative advantages case's popularity seems to come from the difficulty of proving that real and significant damage is inherently caused by the *status quo*. Since no harms are alleged by the affirmative when it uses the comparative advantages case, the negative cannot employ a denial strategy. Since no defects in the *status quo* (except failing to adopt the plan) are cited by the affirmative using this case, the strategy of defending the *status quo* cannot be sensibly employed by the negative.

Nevertheless, there are four ways of countering the comparative advantages affirmative. They are:

1. *The Counterplan.* The negative may offer a counterplan. Of course, the plan must be significantly different from the affirmative's plan, and it must bring all of the benefits of the affirmative's proposal. Additionally, it must bring more benefits but not at the expense of results, workability, or the cost of implementation.

2. *Plan Attack.* The negative may attack the plan in isolation. It may do so in one of two ways. First, they may argue the plan does not represent a genuine change from the *status quo*. Second, the plan has disadvantageous effects overlooked by the affirmative.

3. *Advantages Attack.* The negative may attack the advantages in isolation. This may be done in two ways, either by showing the advan-

tages are not of positive value, or, by proving the advantages are not sufficiently significant to warrant changing the *status quo.*

4. *Causal Relationship Attack.* The negative may attack the causal link between the plan and advantages. This can be done either by denying the advantages will result from the plan, by demonstrating that the advantages can be obtained from the *status quo,* or by proving that the advantages stem not from the plan, rather, they come from an extra-propositional plank of the plan.

Goals-Criteria.

Recently developed, the goals-criteria case requires the affirmative to outline either specific or generally accepted goals within the *status quo,* to establish that a plan is called for because these goals are not met under the *status quo,* to propose a plan, and to assert that the plan would meet the criteria established by the goals. The fundamental difference between a comparative advantages case and a goals-criteria case is the reasoning. In a comparative advantages case, the argument is that implementing the plan would, *post hoc,* give certain benefits. The goals-criteria case, on the other hand, reasons that goals exist, *a priori,* but are unmet by the *status quo,* and that meeting these goals warrants the adoption of the plan.

Because this case is relatively new, there is no standard strategy for the negative. However, there are some generally agreed upon attacks.

1. *Counterplan.* The negative can offer a counterplan.

2. *Goals Attack.* The negative attacks the goals in one or several of these ways: (1) the goal is being met by the *status quo;* (2) the goal is not a true goal of the *status quo;* (3) the goal can be attained through the *status quo;* (4) the goal conflicts with other, more important goals; (5) the goal represents short-sighted thinking and will soon be replaced by long-range goals; and (6) the goal is not new, therefore, it does not represent any real change from the *status quo.*

3. *Criteria Attack.* The negative can attack the criteria in the following ways: (1) the criteria derived from the goal are faulty; they are vague, idealistic, or are not derived from the stated goal; and (2) the criteria are insufficient and must be supplemented by additional goals — goals which would preclude the affirmative's proposal.

4. *Plan Attack.* The negative can attack the plan in one or several of these ways: (1) the plan does not meet the criteria; (2) the plan is no improvement over the *status quo* as it attempts to meet the criteria; (3) disadvantages would result from implementing the plan; and (4) the plan is unworkable.

Up to this juncture, we have outlined the possible negative strategies for three different affirmative cases. The needs-plan-advantages case takes its substance from some harm that exists in the *status quo;* the comparative advantages case takes its substance from the assertion that new advantages will result from its plan; and, the goals-criteria case takes its substance from pre-existing goals which serve as the criteria and warrant for adopting the plan. We have outlined negative strategies for dealing with each. However, the remaining four negative types are simply variations of the three just outlined and need not be detailed extensively.

Alternative Justification.

Because of the alternative justification case's unique structure, that is, several independent plans each with its own advantages, the negative team must alter its speaking responsibilities. Instead of the usual division of labor between the first and second negative speaker, the team must be prepared to refute each of the affirmative alternatives as a separate unit. Also, the negative must condense the attack whenever possible rather than scattering its attention across all of the issues. And, the team must focus on the vital alternatives, dismissing quickly those that require little attention, while attacking in depth the more crucial ones. Yet the negative must refute all alternatives since, theoretically, the affirmative wins if one alternative remains standing.

Like any "shotgun" approach, an alternative-justification case will lack support. The affirmative will not be able to offer much evidence as it develops each alternative. The negative, then, has a distinct advantage and should exploit this lack of support.

Effects-Oriented.

Recall that this type of affirmative basically treats the symptoms instead of the causes of *status quo* problems. The affirmative may use either the traditional or comparative-advantages organization in presenting its effects orientation. The negative, thus, may employ the negative strategies applicable to the traditional or comparative-advantages cases with some adaptations. The negative, for instance, can attack the alleged effects by arguing they do not exist or by proving they are not significant. Causality can be attacked by proving that the alleged effects do not result from the *status quo.* Also, there could be multiple causes for the effects, and, if the affirmative fails to acknowledge them, the negative has grounds for attack.

On-Balance.

Two negative forms of attack — defense of the *status quo* and the counterplan — could be used to refute this case. Since the affirmative focuses specifically on the cost factor of the *status quo,* the first negative approach would be to defend the status quo's alleged high costs as a necessary part of society. As the second alternative, it could suggest a counterplan. The counterplan would alleviate the high costs under attack by the affirmative but retain the other features of the status quo not attacked.

Comparative Need.

This case is not substantively unique, simply a variation of the comparative-advantages type. It argues for a plan and advantages, both of which are designed to prevent some sort of future danger. Since it is a variation of the comparative advantages, the negative strategies for dealing with that case apply to the comparative need.

Case Construction and Development

With the exception of the counterplan approach, all of the possible negative cases in a debate are based first upon direct refutation of the affirmative case. Good negative debating is not canned; it is directly related to the affirmative case it wishes to defeat. Therefore, negative refutation, to be effective, must be organized. The best way to achieve clear organization is to follow the points made by the affirmative in chronological order. In short, the affirmative structure becomes negative-attack structure. The only exception to this is if the affirmative is woefully disorganized. Then, the good negative debater organizes the affirmative case for the opposition, indicating what the major need contentions are, and so forth. Usually, in this situation, the affirmative debaters are thrilled to find that they had a structure, and are pleased to debate on negative terms. Despite the negative's best efforts, however, a poorly-organized affirmative will produce a messy debate. And, often, good negative teams lose messy debates.

The amount of time spent by the negative on running refutation in the constructive speeches depends first upon how much time they will spend on constructive arguments. Usually, each speaker will not exceed four of his ten minutes on his constructive case, so he has six minutes for direct attack. He saves his constructive remarks for last, however, and begins with direct attack. By timing his constructive remarks he knows how much time he has to attack. Usually, the team-mates will divide the constructive time so that each has some prepared remarks, but the first speaker is likely to have a longer set speech than the second speaker. As a matter of fact, he should have a ten-minute speech ready to go in the event of a "history" first affirmative, a trick approach occasionally used by affirmatives. At times, the first affirmative speaker will deliberately say nothing argumentative. Often he merely sketches a history of the problem. The first negative speaker who has no prepared remarks will then be unable to say much more than "He didn't say anything!" This gets rather dull when repeated often in ten minutes. So, the negative must be prepared for this with a speech ready to go. Here is a sample format for organizing the negative constructive speeches.

First Negative Speaker:

I. Salutation.

II. Challenge or request for clarification of definitions (optional, but it must be done at this time, if done at all).

III. Partition and/or statement of negative philosophy (the partition will include the points to be refuted and the constructive remarks that follow).

IV. Running refutation and summary of attack.

V. Summary and appeal for rejection of the resolution.

Second Negative Speaker:

I. Salutation.

II. Continuation of attack on terms (optional).

III. Partition of the fifteen-minute negative "block" (what you will do and what your partner will do in the next speech, his rebuttal).

IV. Running refutation and summary of *your part* of the attack.

V. Constructive case (either rebuild of partner's and/or additional contentions).

VI. Summary and appeal for rejection of the resolution.

Speaker Duties

Like the affirmative speakers, those on the negative have certain broad responsibilities or duties to perform and each of their speeches must fulfill certain general purposes. These duties and purposes follow. In meeting them, negative debaters, of course, need to adapt them to the specific requirements of the case structure they employ.

First Negative Constructive Speech.

Purpose: To establish the negative lines of clash with the affirmative case and to develop the negative case.

Duties: (1) a salutation; (2) a statement of the negative point of view toward the resolution and the first affirmative speech just presented; (3) an acceptance or rejection of the affirmative definition of terms; (4) a statement and refutation of each affirmative issue; (5) the presentation of the negative case, if any; and, (6) a summary.

Remarks: This speech and all of the remaining speeches of the debate must adapt to the preceding ones and clash directly with the opposition's arguments; this speech and the ones that follow cannot be prepared word for word prior to the debate but must be conceived during the debate as the preceding speeches unfold.

Second Negative Constructive Speech.

Purpose: To attack the rebuilt affirmative case.

Duties: By the time this speech begins the entire affirmative case has been stated and the second negative speaker can analyze and refute the complete affirmative case. However, an important point deserves attention: the first negative rebuttal speech immediately follows this speech which allows the negative team fifteen minutes of continuous speaking. Called the "negative block," this fifteen minutes is crucial to the negative. In fifteen minutes the two negative debaters should destroy the affirmative case and most negative debate teams organize their combined time in the negative block to do so.

There are several ways to organize the negative block: (1) the second negative constructive speaker can spend his time attacking the affirmative plan while his partner in the rebuttal speech attacks the issues; or, (2) the second negative constructive speaker can attack the plan and several issues while his partner attacks the remaining issues. Other ways are possible.

Whatever way is used, the second negative constructive speech should include: (1) a salutation; (2) a summary of what the speaker will do in this speech (and what his partner will do in the next if they share the negative block as we recommended); (3) the refutation of plan, needs, or advantages; (4) a summary.

Remarks: A principle of debate is that no new arguments can be introduced in the rebuttal speeches — new evidence and elaboration of arguments are allowed but no new arguments. All of the affirmative and negative arguments must be stated by the end of the second negative constructive speech. Therefore, the negative must have countered all affirmative needs and plan in a general way at least by the start of the rebuttals. It is good strategy for the second negative constructive speaker to announce what the first rebuttal speaker will do since through that announcement he precludes any misconceptions about introducing new arguments in the rebuttals.

First Negative Rebuttal Speech.

Purpose: To continue the negative block attack stated by his partner in the previous speech.

Duties: (1) a salutation; (2) a summary; (3) the continuation of the negative attack; (4) a detailed summary of the entire negative — repeating the highlights of the negative case and the attacks on the affirmative.

Remarks: The final summary should tie together all of the important points covered in the negative block. This speech should hopefully convince the judges that the negative has won the debate.

Second Negative Rebuttal Speech.

Purpose: To answer the remaining issues and summarize the entire debate to demonstrate the superiority of the negative.

Duties: The speaker should spend all of his time on summing up the debate by (1) explaining how each affirmative issue has been attacked and how and why each issue does not stand; (2) rebuilding the negative case for the last time; and (3) stressing the negative strengths.

Remarks: This speech concludes the negative's part of the debate so it must once again shift the burden of rebuttal back to the affirmative. The speaker should emphasize the affirmative errors and omissions, leaving the impression that the opposition was successfully defeated.

7

Refutation and Rebuttal

Debate occasionally is likened to a battle between opposing armies as the two teams, affirmative and negative, figuratively clash in combat, only it is verbal combat with words substituting for bullets. Each team, like the opposing armies, attacks the opposition and defends itself. As in a war, attack and defense in debate consume a major share of the action and are vital to winning.

Although we call "attack" refutation and "defense," rebuttal, their functions roughly correspond to the functions of attack and defense in military operations. Refutation is the process of attacking the opponent's arguments for the purpose of weakening, ripping apart, or destroying them. Rebuttal, on the other hand, is the process of defending, strengthening, and rebuilding the arguments attacked by the opposition.

Basic to effective refutation and rebuttal is knowing the critical weaknesses in the opposition's case, as well as in your own. Attacking the opposition's weaknesses is the essential function of refutation. Preparing defenses for your own case's weaknesses, in the event they are attacked, is the essential function of rebuttal. Refutation and rebuttal, therefore, are not spontaneous actions to be considered while the debate is in process. They require special planning, long before the debate starts, and they depend upon thorough research which is based on sound analysis of the proposition.

Experienced debaters, as they are researching the proposition, prepare sets of refutation and rebuttal cards for every possible argument involved in the debate. With these cards they are fortified with an attack or defense for virtually every important point they hear from the opposition. Of course, such preparation is limited by the time available before the debate and by the debater's desire to succeed. Nevertheless, the secret to potent refutation and rebuttal is adequate preparation.

Refutation

There are numerous ways to attack or refute an argument. We will consider attacks on reservations, evidence and reasoning, and, finally, we list general types of fallacious arguments and the techniques to refute them.

Reservations.

Areas vulnerable to attack in a debater's case are the "reservations" or exceptions to the conclusions or claims he makes in his arguments. These exceptions may make the claims false, weak, or irrelevant. As we remember, a "claim" is a conclusion drawn from the specific evidence based upon a relationship created by the debater's use of warrants.

Very few claims in debate are completely beyond challenge. In debate, the subject matter usually treats of probable truth rather than certain truth and debater's claims are almost ways probability statements. For example, let's suppose a debater claims that Joe DiMaggio will win the batting championship in 1980. He derives this conclusion from the evidence at his disposal. The claim deals with probable truth, not certainty, since the claim was made prior to 1980. Numerous events— exceptions — could take place to prove the claim false. DiMaggio may draw many intentional walks and not qualify for the batting title because he did not have sufficient official times-at-bat. He may suffer an injury and be out of action. Another player may enjoy a hitting streak and surpass him. He may retire, and so forth. These exceptions are known as "reservations" in argument, and provide fertile ground for the opposition to attack.

Unfortunately, debaters rarely state the reservations to their arguments, in fact, we caution debaters against making the opposition aware of the exceptions. Rather, we suggest that one of two courses of action be followed: (1) Should the reservation be unimportant to the claim, concede it, that is, admit the reservation is true and show how unimportant it is; and (2) Should the reservation be important, remove the argument from the case whenever possible and avoid its defeat.

Many arguments cannot be conceded or removed in spite of their reservations, and one of the debater's tasks is to locate those exceptions which may make arguments false, weak, or irrelevant. Consequently, all arguments worthy of inclusion in a debate should be analyzed to determine if they contain possible reservations.

Figure 1 presents an illustration of a negative attack on an affirmative claim, with the attack developed around the reservations to the claim. In the illustration the affirmative advances what seems to be a sound argument — in fact, the United States Congress believed so strongly in the claim, it created the Reorganization Act. The argument deals with probable truth; no one could possibly know for certainty that the Act would lead to a fast, efficient, low-cost postal service. The reservations to the claim make it weak and ripe for negative attack. As the negative proves, a modern, mechanized postal service does not reduce costs, it increases them, partially because of mis-sent letters and machine-damage to parcels. Bargaining fails to provide realistic wages and performance standards, the negative shows. And, business is using other forms of delivery. The negative refutes the affirmative claim by attacking the reservations to the claim.

Of course, the affirmative has a similar course of action open to it. The affirmative can attack the negative's reservations since they, too, deal with probabilities. No one knows whether the mechanical failures are only temporary and, once cleared-up, costs will drop. Nor do they know wages will not level off and performance will increase. With increases in telephone and telegraph rates, people may once again turn to letter writing as their principal form of communication.

Both teams, affirmative and negative, have to be so well prepared they will know all of the possible reservations to their arguments and have defenses for them.

Refutation of Evidence.

Evidence consists of tangible objects, opinion, factual examples, and statistics, with the last three most commonly used. Certain tests can be applied to evidence to evaluate its validity. Since evidence is one of the debater's strongest weapons to support or prove his arguments, every piece of evidence should be tested to determine whether it is false, weak or irrelevant. Invalid evidence, of course, can weaken or destroy an argument, and the application of the tests to an argument can point out the invalid data.

Figure 1. Attacking a Claim through its Reservations

Affirmative Argument

DATA

The Postal Reorganization Act of 1970 gives the U.S. Postal Service broad powers to run its own affairs: to borrow money to modernize, to bargain with labor, to price its services itself.

↓

WARRANT

Independent of Congressional interference, the Postal Service would operate like a private business and pay for itself.

↓

CLAIM

The Postal Service will provide fast, efficient, low-cost postal service under the new Act.

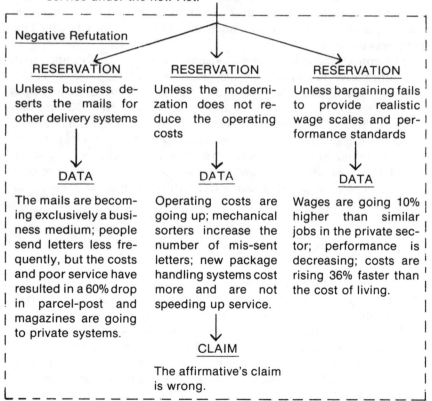

Negative Refutation

RESERVATION	RESERVATION	RESERVATION
Unless business deserts the mails for other delivery systems	Unless the modernization does not reduce the operating costs	Unless bargaining fails to provide realistic wage scales and performance standards

↓ DATA ↓ DATA ↓ DATA

DATA	DATA	DATA
The mails are becoming exclusively a business medium; people send letters less frequently, but the costs and poor service have resulted in a 60% drop in parcel-post and magazines are going to private systems.	Operating costs are going up; mechanical sorters increase the number of mis-sent letters; new package handling systems cost more and are not speeding up service.	Wages are going 10% higher than similar jobs in the private sector; performance is decreasing; costs are rising 36% faster than the cost of living.

CLAIM

The affirmative's claim is wrong.

1. *Is the evidence relevant to the argument?* For evidence to be of any value in a debate, it must be relevant to the argument in which it is being used and the debater will have to explain the relevance or the evidence will serve no useful purpose.

2. *Is there enough evidence?* Evidence from a variety of sources is important but just how much to use depends on the argument and on the evidence itself. Some arguments need little support. Others are so controversial that they require as much evidence as time permits.

3. *Is the evidence clear and accurate?* Evidence, typically, comes from books or periodicals and, thus, is quoted out of context. That is, a debater cannot read aloud the entire book or magazine article from which the evidence is taken, so necessarily, he reads or paraphrases only that which he thinks has value to his argument. Often he adds in what he believes is the meaning of the quotation. Inaccuracies and lack of clarity could result.

4. *Is the evidence consistent with other evidence?* We are taught early in life to verify the data we hear. However, verification may not be entirely possible since frequently several reports have been written about the same event and each report may be slightly different. If the reports result from proper research and the circumstances surrounding the event have not changed significantly, then one report should approximate the other report. Such reports used as debate evidence would then have some validity. However, if the reports are not consistent with each other, we should be wary of the evidence's validity. Such inconsistent evidence can be refuted simply by pointing out the inconsistencies.

5. *Is the evidence recent?* Generally speaking, the most recent evidence is the best evidence. An excellent reservation to raise about an opponent's evidence, therefore, concerns the recency of it. What might have been true at an earlier time in history may not be true today.

6. *Is the source of the evidence cited?* The source of the evidence should always be completely and clearly stated. The reason is that evidence is dependent for its acceptability on the credibility of its source. If no source is cited, then we must treat the evidence as the asserted opinion of the debater himself. And, the debater's opinion has little credibility with the average judge. An opponent, hearing evidence without the source indicated, has legitimate cause to challenge it.

7. *Is the source of the evidence competent?* The concern here is whether or not the authorities, and the publications named, are known for their competent reporting. The authority must be an expert in the subject matter in order for the evidence to be useful in debate.

8. *Is the source trustworthy?* The source of evidence, whether a person or periodical article, should be one in which people place absolute trust, otherwise the veracity of the evidence is questionable. The feeling

is "if the source is not trustworthy, why should the evidence represent the truth?"

9. *Is the source biased, reluctant, or unconcerned?* Biased sources are apt to have a personal stake in what they report. A Socialist talking about social welfare perhaps will present a biased point of view in favor of his party's stand on social reform. A Communist undoubtedly will be prejudiced in favor of his party's program. Their biases tend to invalidate what they say.

Reluctant and unconcerned sources make better witnesses. Reluctant witnesses are those loath to testify and do so only because circumstances force them to do so. A witness to a murder may be reluctant to testify against the murderer if the witness could be harmed by testifying. However, the court demands the truth and the witness reluctantly tells what he saw. His testimony becomes credible partially due to the threat of harm imposed upon him. Similarly, the testimony of an unconcerned source — one who has nothing to gain by the statement made — has validity.

The debater needs to look for biased sources in the evidence of his opponents and challenge such evidence on the basis of it being a prejudiced source.

Evidence can be attacked, and a large number of debates are won by refuting the opponent's evidence. Therefore, let no important evidence of questionable validity get by without attack.

Refutation of Reasoning.

Attacks should be directed to faulty reasoning, just as they should be made against faulty evidence. Fallacious evidence, however, is reasonably easy to discover and attack if the debater has researched the proposition. Faulty reasoning is more difficult to attack and attack on reasoning requires that the debater understand the relationship of the evidence to the claim in each argument.

The tests should reveal faulty reasoning. The tests applicable to each of the six most common types of reasoning follow.

1. *Causation.* Causal relationship implies that one thing produces another. A good teacher produces a good debater, for example. One thing, however, may not be the only cause, the principal cause, or the real cause of the effect — in the example, good teachers do not necessarily produce good debaters. The following are tests of causal reasoning.

    a. Are the alleged cause and alleged effect directly related? People the world over have tended to assume a cause-effect relationship between the fact that children watch crime movies, see crime on television, and read crime comic books, and the fact that there is a steady increase in juvenile crime. Extensive research studies on the problem have failed to produce a cause-effect relationship. Millions of children continue to expose themselves to movies, books, and television shows with a crime theme yet lead crime-free lives. In this instance, the alleged cause (increased exposure to crime) and the alleged effect (increased crime rate) exist in proximity to one another. Other causes have been shown to be as much or more closely related to the increase in crime.

b. Is the alleged cause the only or the primary cause? Tony Kubek, former star shortstop for the New York Yankees, worked hard as a youth to learn how to play his position. Some who knew him as a youngster attributed his success to his hard work and they tended to argue, "Tony worked very hard; hard work produces stars; therefore, Tony became a star." That causal argument would fail test two. Tony's success could be credited to several causes, not just to hard work. Tony's uncle, who taught him some of the fundamentals, spent many hours a year for many years working with Tony in fielding practice. Tony's coaches — he played on many baseball teams in his youth — helped him learn his position. Tony was highly motivated to play and enthusiastic about sports, especially baseball. Tony was well-equipped physically for the game. A combination of causes produced the effect, in our example, a star shortstop. Many, if not most, effects we observe are produced by a combination of causes.

c. Is the alleged effect the only effect or most important effect? Just as effects can be produced by multiple causes, so can causes produce multiple effects. Kubek's hard work, enthusiasm, and skill produced an effect, a New York Yankee shortstop. But other, perhaps even more important effects resulted from the multiple causes. The knowledge about baseball that Kubek gained led directly to lucrative television and radio contracts as a baseball game broadcaster. But there were several other effects. He earned an excellent salary as a player, and he endorsed products for which he was paid, among other effects.

d. Is the cause capable of producing the effect? This test aims at ascertaining a common error in reasoning, termed "*post hoc ergo propter hoc*" by logicians. This translates "after this therefore because of this" and means that because one event took place after another event occurred, the first event occurring in time caused the second. Winter follows fall. Fall, however, does not cause winter; many other phenomena are responsible.

2. *Sign.* When we reason by sign, we base our reasoning on the close relationship of one thing to another, the presence or absence of the one may be taken as the presence or absence of the other. We see rope tows on the mountainsides and we assume that those are skiing areas. We see a broad green meadow with red flags every few hundred yards and we presume the meadow contains a golf course. Thus, in a sign relationship, two or more things go together and, if one is observed, the existence of the others usually constitutes a justifiable inference — not always, however, as the tests below indicate.

   a. How consistent is the sign? Are cases known in which the presence of one of the things in the sign relationship is not accompanied by the presence of the other? It is often argued that a high gross national product (GNP) is a sign of a high per capita income. Opponents of this argument offer the reservation that Japan has a low per capita income in spite of having one of the world's highest GNP, thus they contend that the GNP is an unreliable sign of a high personal income.

   b. Are there special conditions which make the sign unreliable? Most sign relations generally follow, although under extraordinary circumstances the relationship does not hold.

   c. Is the sign relationship reciprocal? If we look out the window and see snow falling, we can assume that the temperature is below freezing. If the temperature is below freezing, it does not necessarily follow that snow is falling. What this test emphasizes is that sign relationships generally point only in one direction. To suggest the relationship also points in the other direction may be fallacious, as our example demonstrates.

   d. Are there other signs leading to the same conclusion? There may be many sign relationships leading to the claim under consideration, not only one or two. Smoke is not always a sign of fire. Before turning in a fire alarm, check for other signs of fire. Smoke combined with heat may not necessarily indicate fire. Smoke, heat, and a red glow may not either. Flames certainly would be a sign of a fire, although the fire may be under control, like a bonfire at a picnic, and not require firemen to put out. In an argument with a sign relationship, all the relevant signs should be stated, otherwise the argument may not stand.

3. *Analogy*. Arguing on the basis of analogy involves seeking acceptance of claims based on comparison. Hence, we reason if two or more things are alike in one or more respects, they are apt to be alike in other respects. But analogies need to be tested because significant points of dissimilarity usually occur between the things being compared.

    a. Are there significant similarities or differences between the things being compared? If Honolulu and Miami are being compared in terms of climate, the similarities are significant. The temperature, rainfall, sunshine, wind and so on, are quite similar, and a sound argument could be made that climate-wise the two cities compare. In terms of living costs, however, significant differences are obvious. Hawaiians earn more for what they do and pay more for what they buy than most other people in the world. In terms of geographic location, the two cities may appear similar. However, Honolulu sits on a small land mass, the island of Oahu, thousands of miles away from other lands, while Miami sits on a larger land mass. Arguments about Honolulu and Miami based on analogies related to living costs and geographic locations would be fallacious because of the differences.

    b. Are the points of similarity important to the comparison? Miami and Honolulu may be similar in climate, crop growth, and business activity. To conclude from these similarities, therefore, that a resident of Miami would find living in Honolulu similar to living in Miami probably would be fallacious. The Miami resident would discover a different way of life in Honolulu.

4. *Generalization*. One of the more common warrants, generalization is typified by the presence of a limited number of examples, the implied assumption that these examples are universal to the class, and the conclusion that all other members of the class are like those in the examples. Hence, reasoning based on generalizations are concerned with evidence, and the validity of the reasoning rests on the sufficiency of the evidence. The general tests for evidence are applicable to generalization, therefore, and should be used to test generalizations.

5. *Classification*. This type reasons that what is true of a class is also true of all of the members of the class. Arguments based on classification must meet these tests:

    a. Are the class members alike? To be alike, all the members of the class need to have common characteristics. To argue, "Brown is a Socialist, all Socialists support anti-pollution legislation, therefore, Brown is a supporter of anti-pollution legislation," could be fallacious if the opposition could prove that not all Socialists support such legislation. In a political party containing thousands of members, it should not be difficult locating people who are opposed to anti-pollution legislation for some reason or other.

b. Does the class possess the characteristic attributed to it in the reasoning? This test asks for proof that the class actually holds the quality assigned to it — that the Socialists (the class) as a group believe in anti-pollution legislation (the quality).

c. Does the thing identified belong to the class? This test asks "Is Brown an actual member of the Socialist party?" Obviously, if the thing named in the evidence does not belong to the class, the argument would be fallacious.

Miscellaneous Refutation Techniques.

Finally, we mention several special devices which are common in debate:

1. *Table-turning* — when the debater uses the logic or evidence of his opponents to support his case.

2. *Contradictions* — when one opposing speaker says something which actually contradicts his partner's position, or when one opposing speaker contradicts himself. Point this out.

3. *Reading further* — when the debater goes on further with the reading of an opposition evidence source, proving that the opposition quoted it out of context.

4. *Later source* — when the debater shows that the expert quoted by the opposition evidently changed his mind later. Experts sometimes do this. Read the more recent source.

5. *Dilemma* — when the debater develops two possible answers to a problem, each of which damages the opponent's position.

6. *Reduction to the absurd* — when the debater extends an opposing argument to the extreme to illustrate its absurdity.

There are similar devices which we do not recommend because they are invalid. However, they may be used against you, so you should be aware of them:

1. *Shifting ground* — this usually happens when a debater has been rather successful in his refutation of an opposing contention. Later in the debate, the debater discovers that the contention has changed. In this case, his opponents have shifted ground. Ground-shifting is more insidious when the opponents shift emphasis rather than contentions (an insignificant point suddenly becomes "major" after you have refuted the erstwhile "major" points). Ground-shifting is refuted by exposing it.

2. *Name-calling* — attacking a point by attaching a nasty label to it. Refute name-calling by exposing it.

3. *Sarcasm* — a personal attack upon a debater, usually, or his case or his documentation. Don't reciprocate; sarcasm usually defeats itself.

4. *Arguing in a circle* — proving that grass is green because it's grass, and grass is always green. In short, using a part of the conclusion as the argument.

The techniques mentioned so far concern direct attacks on the opponent's arguments. However, it is not always possible to refute an argument directly, even though direct refutation is usually the best kind. Therefore, consider the other ways to refute an argument:

1. *Concede an obvious truism.* Make sure that this concession won't damage your case. Actually, you may choose merely to ignore truisms or obviously fallacious or unsupported points; this still concedes the argument, though not quite so overtly. We recommend that you ignore truisms, but that you at least point out the inadequacy of a fallacious or unsupported argument.

2. *Reject the argument.* When you reject, make sure you clearly state the reasons for your rejection. The rejection can be strengthened when you add evidence which supports your view, thus, making your attack more direct.

3. *Match the argument with one of your own.* This way it may or may not cast doubt as to the strength of the opposing contention, but makes it necessary for the opponents to defeat your argument before theirs will stand.

4. *Minimize the argument.* This technique is a limited concession, but it can be an effective way to show the opponent's exaggeration of a problem which you contend is really insignificant. This is a common negative attack upon affirmative need contentions. It is usually strengthened when the negative uses a repairs case to show how a slightly modified *status quo* will remedy the problem.

In addition to direct refutation, therefore, the debater may concede, reject, match, or minimize an opposing argument. Usually a variety of forms are used in each debate.

Suggestions for Refutation.

1. *Research extensively.* Effective refutation results from a thorough knowledge of the proposition, not from the utilization of tricks or questionable maneuvers. A negative team must be prepared for every possible affirmative case; the affirmative for every possible negative

argument. The team that does the better job of research maintains a distinct advantage in refutation.

2. *Attack important arguments.* Arguments vital to a case must be refuted in some manner, even if the attack is weak. A failure to attack usually means the argument is significant and valid.

3. *Refute whenever possible.* While the first affirmative constructive speaker has nothing specific to refute, the other speakers do, and in their constructive and rebuttal speeches, they must attack.

4. *Keep the opposition on the defensive.*

5. *Construct refutation cards.* Prepare for refutation by constructing refutation cards for each argument. They provide a quick, accurate means of refutation and are a valuable ally.

6. *Organize the refutation.* Effective refutation ordinarily follows these five steps:

    a. State the argument you are going to refute, approximately as your opponent presented it.

    b. Show how the argument relates to your opponent's total case.

    c. State your position — indicate your objection or counterclaim.

    d. Present your argument with its support.

    e. Show the effect of the refutation on your opponent's case.

Rebuttal

Rebuttal engages both affirmative and negative teams since it is the process of rebuilding those arguments refuted by their opponents. Both need to prepare for it by having available additional support for their constructive arguments and by developing arguments to refute the arguments the opposition used against them.

The "burden of rebuttal" concept should be kept in mind during the preparation period. During a debate, the burden of rebuttal will shift from team to team. Once a team's argument is refuted, it has the burden of rebuttal to rebuild it. If the rebuilt argument is refuted, it has to be rebuilt once more. The opposition, of course, has a similar responsibility. When one team or the other can no longer sustain its burden of rebuttal, the other team will carry the argument. Hence, preparation has to be complete, otherwise the burden may not be sustained.

Suggestions for Rebuttal.

1. *Rebuild only the essential arguments.* Unless the opposition has been ineffective in refutation, you may have more to answer than possible

in the time available, especially in the rebuttal speeches. Concentrate, therefore, on rebuilding the arguments vital to your case, although a short comment about those you cannot rebuild completely is always worthwhile.

2. *Avoid reusing evidence.* In rebuttal, produce new evidence; do not use that which you gave earlier unless you need to do so for clarity purposes.

3. *Eliminate the fallacies in your case.* Before the debate, eliminate weaknesses or faulty reasoning in your case to the best of your ability. The best rebuttal comes from the absence of weaknesses.

4. *Relate all rebuttal arguments to your case.* The relationship that your rebuttal arguments have to your case should always be clearly made. A way to do this is to restate the argument as you originally stated it.

5. *Organize the rebuttal.* The steps in rebuilding an argument are similar to those in refuting one, that is:

    a. State the argument as stated in the original speech.
    b. State your opponent's attack approximately as he stated it.
    c. Show the relevance of the argument to your case.
    d. Support your argument with adequate evidence.
    e. Show how the rebuttal affects your case.

8

The Cross-Questioning Process

Question-and-answer argument is one of the oldest forms of discourse, dating back at least 2400 years. In the early years of Western civilization, about the time of Plato, a form of argument called "dialectic" was practiced by scholars and their pupils. Dialectic as it was practiced then proceeded through the use of questions and answers. The examiner and the respondent had to be sufficiently trained and skilled in their roles so that they were able to compete with an equality of experience to establish the probable truth about the subject of their argument.

The question-and-answer method found favor in the courts of the time. The "lawyer" at that time could call witnesses but only he could question them. However, centuries later — in the eighteenth century — this practice was changed. Instead of allowing only the attorney who called the witnesses to question them, the opposing attorney was permitted to cross-examine the witnesses he did not call. As a result, cross-examination became a process that trial lawyers had to master. Subsequently the training in and the practice of cross-examination grew in popularity.

While cross-questioning enjoys a long history, cross-examination debate as an academic exercise is relatively new. Its beginning is attributed to J. Stanley Gray of the University of Oregon who in 1926 originated the Oregon style of debate, a form of cross-examination.

To present an understanding of the cross-examination process, we treat these topics: the goals of cross-questioning and preparation for cross-questioning including the role of the examiner and the role of the witness.

The Goals of Cross-Questioning

The goals of cross-questioning are to clarify, to develop cases, and to refute.

1.   *To clarify.* Frequently debaters present arguments that lack clarity. It is difficult when listening to understand what was said. Cross-questioning makes it possible for the opponents to find out what was meant. Questions such as, "Would you explain what you meant when you said . . .?" or "Would you clarify your second need contention?" should bring answers that will clear up the murky arguments.

2.   *To help develop the questioner's case.* The answers to questions should be used in subsequent speeches, especially when the answers admit problems in the witness's case. But the admissions must be related to specific arguments or to the case analysis so the significance of the admission is demonstrated.

3.   *To help refute the opponent's case.* The opponent's evidence and reasoning can be attacked in a multitude of ways. In orthodox debate, the attacks are made during the constructive and rebuttal speeches. In cross-examination debate, additional time is available, that which comes in the questioning periods. During these periods the questioner can confront his opponent face-to-face and question him specifically about his evidence and reasoning. Questions can be asked about the evidence, its source, the lack of it, and so on. Additionally, questions can be used to expose fallacies, errors, or irrelevancies in an argument.

Types of Questions

There are nine types of questions, each of which has a specific purpose. In this section, we will discuss the types and note which ones can be used to manage more effectively the cross-examination periods for the questioner.

1.   *Open questions.* Open questions are broad and unstructured, simply indicating the topic to be talked about. Normally they allow the respondent to say as much as he pleases and are useful in debate to clarify a previous speaker's remarks. Examples are the two stated above: "Would you explain what you meant when you said . . .?" and "Would you clarify your second need contention?" Both let the respondent take the initiative and make a speech on the subject being asked about. The problem with

asking questions is exactly that — the respondent can make a speech and use up the questioner's time in the process. Because of this, we discourage their use except in the most unusual circumstances, for instance, when the opponent has made such a grevious mistake that allowing him to expound on it will help destroy his case. Well-prepared debaters rarely make such mistakes, hence, we recommend using other types of questions.

2. *Closed questions.* Closed questions call for a response of a very few words, ordinarily one or two. This characteristic makes them extremely valuable to the cross-examiner. He maintains control of the examination when he employs them.

Three variations of the closed question exist — identification, selection, and yes/no. *Identification* questions require a one or two-word answer about some person, place, group, time, number, and so forth. The query comes in the form of who, what, when, where, how many, and which sort of question. Note that the answers to these questions can be given in a word or two: "How old are you?" "What is your name?" "Where were you born?" "When were you born?" "How many children in your family?" Once the answer is given, the questioner has the right to cut-off the respondent should he start to make a speech. Also, the respondent must answer, even if it be only an "I don't know."

The *selection* question forces the respondent to choose from alternatives, that is, he has to choose one of two or more fixed answers, as in these examples: "Do you prefer blondes or brunettes?" "Do you mean this . . ., or, do you mean this . . .?" "Are you talking about nine-year olds, ten-year olds, or eleven-year olds?" Again, the respondent cannot make a speech and has to answer in a word to two.

The *yes/no* question can be answered with either a "yes" or a "no"; nothing else need be said. "Do you smoke?" "Are you twelve years old?" "Will your partner give the plan?" Should the respondent try to qualify the answer, the examiner can demand that a "yes" or "no" be given — no more.

3. *Leading questions.* Leading questions explicitly or implicitly indicate the answer to be given. They "lead" the respondent to the answer desired by the examiner. To illustrate, we cite the same question worded first in a neutral manner then worded as a leading question: (1) "How do you feel about the president's handling of inflation?" (2) "You don't favor the president's inadequate handling of inflation, do you?" Note the neutrality disappears in the second version and the question provides a direction the respondent can easily take. In its form as a leading question, the respondent is directed to answer, "No, I don't approve." With such an answer, he agrees with the questioner, which the questioner, of course, wants him to do.

Here are additional examples: "Baseball's the grand old game, don't you agree?" "Rain certainly is refreshing, isn't it?" "That movie was simply divine, wouldn't you say?" "You want a safe product for your children's use, don't you?" In each case, the question provides a tempting way to reply. The respondent is lead to a "yes" answer. A "no," on the other hand, would seem contradictory, giving the impression perhaps that the questioner does not know what he is talking about.

Most leading questions tend to distort or bias the respondent's reply and, because they do, they exercise a powerful force in cross-examination. If the expectant tone of the questioner is very impressive and if the person being questioned does not possess great independence and resistance, the inquisitor could very well pack more of his opinion into the witness through the questions than the witness can recall from his knowledge of the facts.

Leading questions are utilized in the "yes-response" technique, a technique devastating in cross-examination when done well. The questioner formulates a series of questions in such a way that the respondent has to agree with them, one by one, and then finds it almost impossible not to agree with the final, key question. Here is an example:

Question: You do believe men and women should receive equal pay for equal work, don't you?
Answer: Yes, I think they should.
Question: And I'm sure you'd agree that they have as much right to a charge account in their names as men?
Answer: I guess they should.
Question: Certainly women should have the right to vote?
Answer: By all means.
Question: And smoke?
Answer: Of course!
Question: Then you obviously favor the Equal Rights Amendment, don't you?
Answer: Well, ah, I guess so.

Once the respondent has said "yes" to the first questions in the series, it becomes difficult to say "no" to the final one. Obviously, a good debater can get out of a trap like this one, but he will have to reply at length to do so and the questioner can stop him before he goes too far.

Open, closed and leading questions are known as *primary* questions. That is, they are used to introduce topics or new areas within a topic in the cross-examination. The next six types are *secondary* questions — questions that elicit more about a topic introduced with a primary question. They could be open or closed in form but they are utilized when answers to primary questions are incomplete, vague, ambiguous, inaccurate, and irrelevant. Their aim is to draw-out more information, to probe an answer and to clarify what was said.

4. *Extension questions.* The extension, also termed the "probe," is useful in obtaining additional information. When the respondent's answers are incomplete or when he does not seem able to put his thoughts into words, the questioner can probe more deeply. For example:

Question: Who says people fear to write?
Answer: Studies say so.
Question: What studies?

The question, "What studies?", is an extension.

Debaters frequently do not want to answer questions that might reveal weaknesses. In such situations, they could be evasive, incomplete, or tentative. Using the extension, the questioner can probe for the correct answers.

5. *Echo questions.* Also called "mirror" or restatements, this form of question replicates exactly or almost exactly what the respondent previously said. It is used to secure more information. For example:

Question: What studies?
Answer: Those of Daly and Miller.
Question: Daly and Miller?

The questioner "echoes" what he just heard, giving it a rising inflection to put it as a question. The technique suggests the questioner is listening so well, he can restate what was said.

6. *Confrontation questions.* This question serves to clarify. At the same time, it can create stress. It usually is employed when the respondent has inconsistencies in his ideas and the questioner wants to clear them up. "Yesterday you said she had blue eyes; today you're not sure. Are they blue or aren't they?" The inconsistency is pointed out in the question and clarification is sought. In cross-examination, the respondent could be made to appear as though he did not know what he was talking about perhaps with telling effect on the judge. For this, confrontive questions are valuable in academic debate.

7. *Direct and Indirect questions.* With the direct question, the debater comes straight out and asks what he wants to know. With the indirect question, the debater infers — beating-around-the-bush, so to speak. Note the difference: (1) "You said when people are apprehensive, they are negatively impacted. What do you mean, negatively impacted?" (2) "You must have some strong feelings about apprehension. Are you suggesting something disagreeable?" In the first version, the questioner states what he wants to know directly. In the second version, he indirectly inquires.

A cross-examiner can lull a respondent into a false sense of security with the indirect approach. His courteous manner and mild way of inquiring could bring admissions the respondent was not planning to make. The "nice guy" image can be a powerful force in cross-examination, especially when the opponent comes on strong.

8.   *Summary questions.* This form of questions provides a simple recapitulation to confirm what was said. If the witness has made several admissions during his testimony, the questioner will benefit by summarizing these for the judge. "Am I correct? You did say that . . . and that . . ., didn't you?"

9.   *Repetition questions.* The questioner simply asks once again what he asked once before when he uses this form of question. He repeats the question because the original answer was vague, evasive or incomplete. "I don't believe you answered the question. I asked, 'Why did it happen?'"

The questioner builds his cross-examination around primary questions — we believe closed and leading questions are best for cross-questioning in debate. The secondary questions are employed as needed during the actual questioning period. Should a primary question be inadequately answered for some reason then the questioner resorts to secondary questions to clarify or to obtain more information.

Preparing for Cross-Questioning

Cross-questioning requires skill, thought, patience, and self-control in addition to a thorough understanding of the debate proposition and an ability to discover the weaknesses in the opponent's case. That sounds like an awesome set of requirements but in actuality the debater should have an excellent command of the proposition by the time he is ready to prepare his cross-examination. By that time, the debater should have analyzed and researched the proposition, constructed affirmative and negative cases, and understand the strengths and weaknesses of all the arguments. The remaining preparation time should be restricted to developing questions and answers.

Developing Questions.

During the preparation period, a series of questions should be drafted for each of the probable issues of the debate. The questions should be designed so that the responses are brief. The questioner wants to be in command of the cross-examination period and should not let the respondent take over. With questions like the "open" type, the respondent might dominate the period, picking up a favorable audience reaction in the process. Therefore, closed questions probably are the best with a mixture of "identification," "selection" and "yes/no" questions being used. Worthwhile, also, are leading questions, especially in the "yes-response" series. However, care must be taken with such a series. An alert opponent will avoid the trap the series is supposed to set.

The questions should elicit admissions and contradictions or point up weaknesses that the questioner can gain some advantage from in later speeches. Hence, there ought to be a clear purpose for the questions or objectives that the questioner tries to reach.

For example, imagine that the proposition, "Resolved, that the Pacific Basin countries should develop a federation of Pacific States," was being debated. The objectives might be to seek from the opponents agreement on these points: (1) the powers necessary to be given to a central government to run the federation; (2) possible dangers to the territories, states, and countries in the Pacific which would necessitate a federation; (3) the threat that Communist nations may unite and harm Pacific Basin countries; (4) the importance of the Pacific defense of the USA, Korea, the Philippines, and Japan; (5) the failure of the United Nations to prevent armed aggression against member countries; (6) both Japan and the USA are committed already to defend Pacific nations and territories.

Objectives like those just listed should relate directly to the constructive speeches and also with what might be expected in the opposition's case. In order to reach the objectives, a series of primary questions should be worked up for each, yet during the actual examination, secondary questions may have to be added.

Several methods are available to organize the series of primary questions. The "funnel" sequence begins with topics that are broad and not objectionable to the respondent. Then, the questions become more and more restrictive as the series continues, closing with the key question, as in the "yes-response" technique of asking leading questions. The "tunnel" or "string-of-beads" sequence in a series of questions of the same type, usually permitting little probing. With the "tunnel," the goal is not in-depth examination of a particular topic but rather the aim is a general examination of many topics. There also is the "yes-response" technique described earlier, useful to direct the respondent's answers to a desired end.

Whatever the questions may be, the questioner must know the answers before asking them. Should the respondent refuse to give the correct answer to a question, the questioner can provide it and, in the process, weaken the respondent's testimony. Should the questioner not know an answer and the respondent does, and it is a strong point in the respondent's favor, the questioner will be in trouble. Thus, the cardinal rule in questioning is, "Know the answers to the questions you ask."

The questions should contain a simple, clear request for delimited information. To test their wording, we suggest they be tried out in practice debates. Then, if they are found to be too long, ambiguous or confusing, they can be rewritten.

Recognize that a statement or two may be needed to introduce the questions. For example: "You said the price of airbags is too high and that there is competition between companies. If there is competition, wouldn't that prompt the manufacturers to lower prices?" The introductory statement, in this case, is necessary to set the stage for the question which follows.

During the actual cross-examination, the questioner must avoid asking questions about points irrefutable even though such questions are on the list. An attack on unassailable points will accomplish little for the questioner. Instead it could emphasize the strength of such points. Likewise, when the questioner wins a point, he should not gloat over it during the exam period. The time to discuss the issue is in the next constructive or rebuttal speech.

During the debate, the questions prepared earlier should be adapted to the opponent's arguments. It may be necessary to add a secondary question or two because of a tactic taken by the opposition and, of course, during the debate, secondary questions requesting additional information or clarification most likely will have to be asked.

The Questioner's Role.

The questioner's role revolves around both the application of acceptable questioning procedures as well as the handling of various types of witnesses. Above all, the questioner must be reasonable, cooperative, eager to please, and courteous. He should establish an atmosphere of cordiality and friendliness in the questioning period, rather than one of hostility and unpleasantness. The effective questioner never arouses opposition by attacking the witness but disarms him by a quiet and courteous manner as he asks his questions.

These suggestions may be helpful in fulfilling the questioner's role:

1.   Control the time; don't let the witness give lengthy answers. Be in command of the questioning period.

2.   Ask fair and relevant questions.

3.   Don't comment on the answers or argue with the witness.

4.   Introduce and conclude the examination period; don't let the witness do so.

5.   Face the audience and talk to them, not the witness.

6.   Speak distinctly and loud enough to be heard.

Developing Answers.

The preparation of the witness has to be more general than that of the examiner. The witness is at the mercy of the examiner since he has only a rough idea of what the examiner will ask. However, the witness should have additional evidence on hand to back up any statements he made in his constructive speech and also some telling evidence to introduce in regard to claims likely to be made by the examiner. Then he takes advantage of any opportunity to use the evidence.

If you know your case well enough as a witness, you should not be surprised by any appropriate question. You should have analyzed the case so carefully that you would know what questions to ask about your case if you were the questioner. And, you should know the answers to every one of the questions.

The examining period belongs to the questioner, and he directs the line of questioning to be pursued. The possibility may occur, therefore, for an unorthodox series of questions. Practice debates with fellow squad members can be useful in this regard, especially when the examiner is asked to prepare a series of trick questions for practice purposes. The witness will not be perplexed when confronted with a similar series in the actual debate. Remember that trick questions rarely, if ever, win debates. If the witness performs his role as we indicate below, he should overcome the handicap of the unorthodox questions.

The Witness's Role.

The questioning period belongs to the examiner. Nevertheless, the witness has certain rights and privileges as well as obligations that are a part of his role. They are: (1) the witness must answer directly and briefly all legitimate questions; (2) he cannot question the examiner except to ask for clarification; (3) he cannot use stalling tactics; (4) he may refuse to answer tricky or unfair questions; (5) he cannot consult his partner; (6) he can admit ignorance; and (7) he should address the audience.

Occasionally we see debater behavior that subverts the goals of cross-questioning. In some instances, such behavior is the result of ignorance on the part of the debater. His intent may not be to harass or personally attack his opponent, although his behavior would lead one to believe that this is so. He simply is not aware that his behavior is unorthodox.

What behavior is improper during cross-questioning periods? The actions listed next are at odds with the goals of cross-questioning.

1. Cross-questioning periods should not be used to attack the opponent's personal integrity. Attack evidence and reasoning but not the debater as a person.

2. The periods should not be used to present arguments. These periods are for questions and answers, not for developing arguments.

3. They should not be used for personal display. An occasional questioner will perform like an actor on the stage in a courtroom scene shouting at the witness, strutting back and forth, gesturing wildly as he tries to act out the part of a great criminal lawyer. Such behavior should be avoided.

4. They are not times for trickery. Cross-questioning should be handled honestly and fairly; "tricks" should be avoided. In fact, we know of no tricks that are effective, and we have watched dozens of cross-questioners trying to get the best of their opponents by gimmicks of some sort. There are no "tricks of the trade" that work. What really is effective is superior research, analysis, organization, case construction, and carefully prepared questioning periods.

9

Debate Behavior: Delivery, Listening, and Ethical Practices

To possess a defensible case, arranged in a meaningful sequence, and worded accurately, clearly, and conversationally is not enough for effective debate. Countless debates are lost because of flaws in the delivery of otherwise well-prepared cases. Countless others are won because verbal restatement or amplification, vocal inflection, or gesture insured against possible distortion of the speaker's data.

We are not suggesting that the debater's delivery is something apart from his speech. We are suggesting that listeners form notions about debaters on the basis of whatever information is available to them. Obviously one source of information comes from the speech itself. The sources of evidence he cites, the depth of analysis he reveals, the persuasiveness of the case he develops — all of which are communicated in the content of the speech — assist the listener to create an impression of the credibility of the debater.

These are not the only sources of information available to the listener to use in building an image of the debater. Throughout the debate, the listener constantly modifies and rebuilds his impression of the debater on the basis of the way the debater talks. Research data supports our belief that effectiveness in delivery contributes not only to the credibility of the debater, but also to his persuasiveness in achieving acceptance of his message. Important to debaters, therefore, is the realization that delivery contributes to the listener's evaluation of the debating, particularly in terms of credibility and persuasiveness. Of course, the impressions a listener gets may be entirely wrong, and first impressions often are. But first impressions tend to be very clear impressions, most listeners tend to get similar impressions, and these impressions tend to exert considerable influence over the judge's evaluation of the debating skills.

Vocal Behavior

Certain characteristics of delivery produce similar sorts of impressions in a wide range of listeners. Those related to rate, volume, pitch, and vocal variety seem to influence listeners' judgments.

Recognizing that in the normal debate the effect of rate will be influenced by the other factors of delivery, that it may not be the sole criterion on which the debater's delivery is judged, we recommend that rate be varied to achieve clarity and emphasis in content. By varying rate, we mean that for the key ideas or for the difficult material in a debate speech, for example, the debater's definitions of terms, the rate be significantly slower than for other less complex material. In other words, for clarity's sake, slow down when presenting difficult ideas, and for the sake of emphasis, slow down when presenting key ideas, otherwise, maintain an average rate of about 175 w.p.m. The debater must be heard. He needs to speak loud enough so that his message will reach all of the people listening to him, without speaking so loud that his volume becomes distracting. Just how loud depends upon room size, noise in the area, and the number of people present. If the room is large and filled to capacity, the debater may have to speak abnormally loud, especially if outside noises filter in to the room. If the room is small, he probably can speak in his normal volume. If the room is large with one listener, the judge, in addition to his fellow debaters, with the judge sitting in the back of the room, the debater will have to speak louder than usual.

Volume, like rate, can be used to emphasize important points. By slightly increasing volume when a key idea is discussed, that idea will stand out.

Pitch refers to the highness or lowness of the vocal tone, and, perhaps the impression pitch instills most in a listener is the impression of strength. A low-pitched male voice, for example, seems to reflect a strong, healthy man while a high-pitched one gives an impression of a skinny weakling. A low-pitched female voice creates an image of a husky, muscular woman, an image most women do not wish to convey. Low-pitched female and high-pitched male voices tend to distract attention from the message.

We have said that rate and volume are effective devices to use in emphasizing words, phrases, and ideas. Pitch can be varied also for purposes of emphasis, and sound duration — the length of time given to the utterance of each sound unit in a word — has emphasis value, too. Emphasis, stress, flexibility, and animation are associated with vocal variety, and variety, which a preponderance of available evidence affirms, is an essential of good delivery.

Vocal variety oftens leads to an impression of liveliness, interest, and well-being. The monotonous voice carries negative feelings of lifelessness, dullness, and unhappiness, and the debater whose voice gives such feelings is so categorized. When there is an absence of vocal variety, the debater often is thought to be uninterested in his topic.

We stated earlier than an audience's impressions of a debater based on his vocal cues frequently will be wrong. The crucial point, however, is not the fallaciousness of the impressions but the fact that the impressions were made in the first place. Listeners do judge a debater's effectiveness on vocal cues. Additionally, the listener's judgment usually occurs unconsciously — he is not aware that he evaluates a debater on the basis of vocal cues. He simply decides that the debater is dull or lively, self-assured or unsure, strong or weak, and responds accordingly. Fortunately, a compensating factor operates: moderately poor vocal quality, poor pitch patterns, non-fluency, and even stuttering do not interfere greatly with comprehension even though they create unfavorable impressions. So, in spite of a poor voice, the debater may be understood. Furthermore, voice is not solely responsible for the image the debater creates. Other aspects of delivery, notably visible behaviors like gestures, posture, and facial expressions, play a part.

Visible Behavior

Unless the listener hears the debate over the radio or via a recording, or reads it in printed form, bodily action cues will influence his conception of the debater. As in the case of the vocal cues, the listener probably will not be consciously aware of judgments based on bodily cues, although occasionally these actions can be so distracting that the listener will notice nothing else.

A common practice among people of all cultures is to begin to determine a stranger's worth on the basis of his appearance. Tallness and shortness, style of clothing and hair, directness of eye contact, speed of movement, all of these and many other similar cues contribute to our decision about a stranger's trustworthiness, friendliness, confidence, intelligence, and so forth. To illustrate, a debater waiting to speak is subjected to that sort of decision-making as he sits, slouches, leans, or slumps at his desk listening intently, yawning, grimacing, whispering, or sneering, while his opponent speaks. When he speaks, his posture, eye-contact, and gestures also are evaluated. Does he lean on the podium, or stand tall? Is he relaxed, or tense? Does he gesture naturally, or do his gestures call attention to themselves? Does he look at his audience, or does he avoid the audience's gaze? The debater who stands tall, appears relaxed, gestures naturally, and looks at his audience more likely produces a pattern of visible behavior consistent with an image of a responsible, confident, sincere person interested in speaking with his listeners.

Despite the fact that quick judgments are made, only on rare occasions is a debater's delivery judged to be so poor that it causes an audience to change an earlier established favorable impression of him. On the contrary, delivery has its greatest impact on the unknown debater, the beginner who has never debated much before or the experienced debater about whom the audience knows little. In those circumstances where the audience forms its initial judgment of the debater from his speech, delivery plays a prominent role. Then, delivery is noticed before the content of the speech has been sufficiently developed to provide a basis for judgment. If the delivery is lively, assured, and direct, the listener's first impression of the debater will be that he is lively, assured, and direct, and he will be judged accordingly. If the delivery is dull, inhibited, and unassured, the content of the speech will have to be remarkably better than that of the opposition in order to overcome those deficits of delivery.

Listening

Debaters share the speaking time. In the typical academic debate, each debater is on his feet talking only one-fourth of the time. What does he do the rest of the time? He listens, and takes notes. Three-fourths of the average debater's time, hence, is spent listening — and note-taking — not sleeping, resting, or thinking about other things.

This time is crucial to the debater's success. As he listens, he learns what his opponents have to say, and, as he listens to what they say, he has to figure out what to say in response to his opponents' remarks. As he listens, he prepares his refutation and rebuttal. Should he be on the negative, he needs to determine what kind of affirmative case he is hearing and to plan the negative strategy to it. The affirmative has to decide what the negative strategy is as it is being orally expounded so that the affirmative can properly reply. The listening time, therefore, has to be used well.

How can the time be best used? Almost all debaters take notes as the debate unfolds. By that we mean, they record what they hear said by their partner and their opponents. By their partner so that they know exactly what he does say. Should he commit an error, miss an important point of the opposition, or contradict what his teammate said, then the necessary adjustments can be made. By the opponents so they know exactly what the opposition's strategy is and what to refute and to rebuild. Debaters need, therefore, to record the whole flow of the debate.

The process of note-taking — in debate jargon it is called "flow-sheeting," "flowing," or "flowing the debate" — is one of the most difficult tasks for beginners to learn. Keeping accurate records of what is being said is necessary for useful analysis and the following suggestions may help.

There are two common methods of note-taking used by debaters. The first is sometimes called the "split-page" technique. Using this technique, you draw a vertical line down four sheets of standard-size notebook or typewriter paper, dividing each page roughly into two equal sizes. On the first sheet, left side, you will present the remarks of the first affirmative speaker, attempting to outline them accurately so you can get the main points clearly. Record some of the evidence sources used or anything else that you may want to comment upon later. If you were the first negative speaker, you could now use this outline as part of the notes for your speech. If you were the second negative speaker, carefully outline what your partner had to say in response to the first affirmative speech in the right column of your notes, opposite your transcript of the first speech. Some debaters then encircle points which were not attacked well, or draw through points which were solidly refuted. Adopt any system you choose, but the important thing is to always have a clear picture of what is happening to the arguments in the debate. Devote page two of your notes to the two second constructive speeches. Put the first rebuttal speeches on page three and the final rebuttal speeches on page four.

The second common note-taking method is quite similar to the first. Rather than using four individual sheets, however, this system uses only one. The sheet must be large. Some debaters use long yellow legal pads; others use artists' paper. On this one sheet is recorded the same information we described previously, with vertical lines drawn down the sheet to delineate different speeches. This sheet has eight columns, and is a record of the entire debate.

Vital to effective delivery is listening — and note-taking. Time wasted while the opposition or your partner speaks is time lost. The average debate is compacted into a short time span and the time available must be used to your advantage.

Unfavorable Practices

By this point it should be clear that listening and delivery through its components of voice, bodily action, and appearance play a role in effective debate as does the content of the debate speech. Our discussion so far has largely been general, especially for delivery, since we have described delivery problems without recommending practices which if followed may eliminate these problems. Some textbooks, in fact, establish sets of rules for behaving orally and visibly in debate. These rules are nonsense, for they fail to account for the different situations in which debate occurs and for the enormous range of behaviors appropriate in each of these situations.

What we can offer in place of a set of rules is a list of debate practices which a vast number of debate coaches believe create an unfavorable impression of a debater. Some of these practices relate specifically to matters of delivery, others deal directly with content, and a few are mixed, dealing both with matters of delivery and content.

Nineteen practices are considered by the coaches to be ones that suggest a debater who lacks credibility and trustworthiness, one who may resort to highly questionable practices for the sole purpose of winning a debate.

1. Debaters or coaches listening to potential opponents and recording their cases to obtain advance information for later use.

2. Either team introducing a new issue in the rebuttal.

3. Breaching normal courtesy, such as heckling, grimacing or loud whispering while opponent is speaking.

4. Citing opinion or fact out of context in which they were written.

5. Fabricating evidence.

6. The affirmative defining the terms of the resolution in such a way as to give them a competitive advantage not inherent in the resolution.

7. The affirmative waiting to answer important issues until the final affirmative rebuttal.

8. Injecting personalities into the debate.

9. The witness taking unnecessary time in answering questions in cross-examination debate.

10. The witness conferring with colleague in cross-exam before asking or answering a question.

11. Using sarcasm.

12. The negative waiting to present a counterplan until the second negative constructive.

13. Debating the debate after the debate with the judge or opponents.

14. Using personal letters as evidence.

15. Using cases prepared by the coaching staff.
16. Using a first affirmative constructive speech written by the coach.
17. Using research materials gathered by the coaching staff or speech classes.
18. Using profanity.
19. Sharing flow sheets of opponent's debates with other schools.

The following sixteen practices, say the coaches, reflect a poor debater, one who is unskilled or incompetent in debating.

1. Either the affirmative or the negative failing to adapt to the opponents' arguments.
2. Either the affirmative or the negative using what is referred to as the "shotgun" case, *i.e.*, offering many arguments with little support in an attempt to gain an advantage over the opponent.
3. Substituting emotional appeals for argument on a specific issue in the debate.
4. Failing to identify sources of information given in the debate.
5. Failing to demonstrate qualifications of authorities quoted.
6. Quoting from obviously prejudiced sources.
7. The affirmative failing to present a *prima facie* case in its constructive speeches.
8. The affirmative defining the terms of the resolution in such a manner that they are vague and unclear.
9. The negative quibbling with the definition of terms without showing valid support for their disagreement.
10. The affirmative failing to present a plan on a resolution that is not clear without a stated plan.
11. The affirmative waiting to present the plan until the very end of the second affirmative constructive speech.
12. Asking tricky and/or leading questions in cross-exam.
13. Debaters using canned speeches after the first affirmative.
14. Bombarding the opposition with a series of oral questions, all of which obviously cannot be answered in the allotted time.
15. The first affirmative constructive speaker presenting a historical or philosophical background to the proposition without touching need which the second affirmative constructive speaker presents.
16. Using the "spread."

The list is by no means exhaustive; other practices can be added which create unfavorable impressions of the debater. The list does note those practices widely considered to be detrimental to a debater's image. Hopefully its inclusion here will stimulate you to evaluate your debating behavior in order to determine what kind of impact it has on others.

To be fair in our evaluations of debaters, we should take into account, also, the variables of intent, degree, and circumstance. To judge a debater as a liar or cheater because he cited opinion out of context may be too harsh if he is merely ignorant of debate procedure as in the case of many beginning debaters. If, on the other hand, his intent is deliberately to deceive or lie, then he should be penalized for his behavior.

The degree or number of times a poor practice occurs also should be considered. If the practice occurs once or twice, it may be overlooked. If it repeatedly takes place, penalties should be imposed.

Likewise, the circumstances surrounding the alleged malpractice need to be reviewed. To save a life, it may be wise to lie, in real life, at least. In academic debate, lying is never justifiable under any circumstances.

Perhaps at this juncture, it may be fruitful to remind ourselves just what academic debate is. It was conceived to be and remains an educational activity. Its primary purpose is to train students to become more effective speakers than they presently are, and, consequently, more effective participants in a democratic way of life.

Although academic debate has been organized along procedures common to much real-life debate, it is usually thought of as a planned curricular or co-curricular activity which observes educationally defensible methods and provides many educational benefits. It strives to get students ready for a life which normally involves a variety of communication experiences.

Academic debating equates substantive speaking in many respects. It pits student against student in friendly advocacy as speaking in real-life pits person against person in all sorts of on-the-job competitive communication situations. Like in real life, in academic debate, instances of misconduct are rare. When they do occur, they seem to result from a desire during the heat of competition to win above all else, much as unethical practices in real life occur when an unreasonable need to succeed prevails over normal ethical behavior.

Unethical conduct happens when the outcome of a single debate becomes so vital that the debater momentarily forgets the purpose behind academic debate. Winning is important; is signifies an instant of educational success. But cheating to win represents a lesson unlearned, a goal not reached. Participation is most important, the instructional benefits which accrue far outweigh a win, or a loss.

10

Judging the Debate

We ended the last chapter by emphasizing the educational goals of academic debate. To begin this chapter, we shall stress the judge's role in the learning process. The judge's evaluation underlies much of the learning actually occurring in debate. Without his judgment, debaters would be forced to guess at how well they did and what they need to do to improve further. The judge provides the evaluation necessary for improvement. Hence, the judge plays an important part in debate; he is the debater's instructor or coach for the moments they are together. He is the "teacher" whose task it is to evaluate the debating, render a judgment, and offer suggestions for upgrading performance — all in a few minutes.

Quite a burden is placed on the judge in order to provide debaters with meaningful and accurate feedback. Judging a debate presents difficulties. The judge has eight speeches to evaluate in orthodox debate, twelve in cross-examination, and the speeches are not separate entities but parts of an organic whole. Each speech relates to those preceding it and each must be criticized in terms of this interrelationship. Additonally, in a debate tournament, the judge usually judges multiple debates, often hurrying to each, and each debate differs from the others, if not in form, certainly in content.

Complaints about a judge's decision are heard frequently — losers occasionally excuse their defeats by blaming the judge. Unquestionably, unqualified persons do judge, not necessarily of their own choosing. They are pressed into service by tournament directors who are short of judges and need "warm bodies" urgently. Be that as it may, the fact is few debate judges are of low caliber; the largest majority are well-prepared to render judgments in debate and do so ably.

Academic debate tournaments are unlike most ordinary speaking situations. They present complications that affect the judging process, such as the ones we just mentioned — the eight interrelated speeches and judging multiple rounds. Besides the ones mentioned, there are other factors impinging on the judge's ability to evaluate. Certain factors appear in the debate setting, certain ones reflect the debaters' speaking behavior, and certain ones affect the judge's diagnostic ability. To recognize that these factors exist should be helpful to the debater in understanding the judge's role in this educational activity. Equally important, the debater should know the criteria, standards, or bases on which a debate is judged. Next, we present the factors and criteria.

Factors Affecting the Judge

The judge's diagnostic and analytical behavior varies from day to day, from setting to setting, from speech to speech. The judge is affected by the rooms, light, noise, fatigue, physical ailments, evaluation tools, and other distracting forces. For example, we judged a debate on a December Saturday when the room was so cold, our judgment was impaired, not to mention the debaters' speaking. In another instance, the final championship round in a debate tournament had seven judges, four representing one of the competing teams' school. Fortunately that team did such a poor job debating, the decision obviously had to go to their opponents, and it did.

The factors affecting the judge's decision may be grouped into five general categories:

1. **Attention span**. How long can the judge listen without becoming fatigued? One hour? Two? More?

2. **Knowledge**. What does the judge know about the type of debate he is judging? What does he know about the tournament's rules and procedures? Is he qualified to judge?

3. **Emotional state**. Can he listen objectively and withhold his decision until all the facts are in? Does the judge make hasty decisions based on incomplete facts?

4. **Perceptual habits**. Does he see what he wants to see? Does he hear and see only that which he believes? Is he excessively influenced by his biases?

5. **Physical state**. Is he tired? Sick? Have a physical ailment which could impair his judgment?

These questions should make it clear that many factors influence the person who judges contest speaking. From the debater's point of view, it is desirable for the judge to be aware of the particular factors that are likely to affect his evaluation and be able to adjust to them. If the judge knows, for example, that after one debate he needs a rest, he should get that rest before judging again. If the judge knows he dislikes long-haired males, he should make adjustments to move his scoring to greater objectivity each time he confronts a long-haired male contestant.

Factors in the Debater's Speaking Behavior

Just as the judge's behavior varies from time to time, so does the debater's. Just as the judge is affected by rooms, light, noise, fatigue, and other distractions, so is the debater. Even in a single debate, his behavior may change. At the start, the voice may be tense and inflexible and the posture rigid and unnatural. Later, as he relaxes, the tension washes away, and he becomes more flexible in voice and posture. In a debate, concentration is required as the contestant listens to his opponents and prepares refutation, and after too much of such effort, fatigue may set in resulting in a loss of fluency when it is his turn to speak.

The tournament presents even more occasion for variation in speaking behavior. A debate tournament may involve five or more debates in the span of a day or two. The constant pressure to adjust to new speaking conditions as the debater moves from round to round is taxing. In each debate, he faces a different team with a different case and confronts a different judge in a different room. Adaptation to these varying circumstances takes skill and stamina.

Like the judge, the contestant's speaking is affected by certain factors, ones almost identical to those listed for the judge. The contestant is affected by his attention span, knowledge, emotional state, physical condition, and perceptual habits.

The judge should be alert to these factors in speaking behavior and take them into consideration when writing his suggestions for improvement. He should know that in the final round the contestants after a day of speaking may not be as good as they were earlier in the day and, therefore, he should temper his criticism accordingly. Likewise, he should recognize that novice debaters, that is, those who are taking part in debate for the first time, will need to be handled differently than experienced ones. The beginners may require more encouragement and less detailed analysis. The old timers probably want a detailed critique which thoroughly analyzes their speaking.

Factors in the Setting

Many factors in the setting could affect the judge's judgment as well as impair the debater's performance. They can be classified into four groups.

1. **Noise in the setting.** Included in this group are a great variety of factors which impair or influence the judge's reception of the debater's speaking. Because of them, the judge gets a distorted version of what the speaker said. These factors are labeled "noise," even though they may not necessarily be discordant sounds disturbing the atmosphere. Rooms that are too hot or cold, that are filled with stale or smoky air fall into this group, if they hinder the judge's reception of the speech. For example, we judged a contest during a "smog alert" period. The polluted air caused us difficulty in concentrating on what was being said. Several audience members, in fact, fainted from the obnoxious fumes. Poor light also may be classified as noise if it impairs vision. The debaters can't see their notes; the judge has to strain to see the debaters, and may miss the impact that facial expression and gestures have on delivery. Uncomfortable seats or a crowded room can be noise if they negatively influence reception. One of the bothersome aspects of a debate we judged was the large audience. The judges were jammed among several hundred audience members in that debate. Each written judgment was noted by the judges' immediate neighbors who whispered it to their neighbors. Noticing this, we withheld writing down our judgments until the contest's end. This delay meant keeping mental records, a difficult task in debate.

2. **Tournament management**. Scheduling four judges from one debate team's school illustrates poor tournament management. But managing tournaments is a difficult task, particularly the scheduling aspects.

Scheduling is a last-minute activity prone to inaccuracies. Scheduling cannot begin until all entries have been received, and then, once a schedule is put together, it remains tentative until the day of the tournament after all the teams have appeared. Students do cancel out, or, do not show up at all, and schedule adjustments have to be made under pressure. Mistakes do occur and errors are inevitable. Yet, many mistakes can be avoided by trained contest managers.

3. **Evaluation tools**. Judges have different diagnostic tools to use in evaluation, such as ballots with a rating scale, checklists, recording instruments, and audience-reaction devices. Each of these tools fulfills only limited purposes and, consequently, there is no perfect evaluation instrument. Each has advantages and disadvantages which the judge should be aware of because they may affect his interpretation of the contestant's performance. For example, the more popular form of debate ballot includes a rating scale and space for written comments. Unfortunately, the rating scale does not give a precise measure of the debater's

ability. It lacks reliability and validity. The judge's written feedback to the debater as a result may lead to misunderstandings between the judge and debater when that type of ballot is employed.

4. **Rules and regulations**. Well-organized tournaments usually have rules and regulations by which they are governed. These cover many items: the criteria of judgment, the proposition to be debated, the length of each speech, time-keeping procedures, contest etiquette, and penalities for failure to comply with the rules. Most of these affect the judge's decision. For example, most tournaments have a rule similar to this one: "A speaker who fails to appear at a debate round within five minutes of the designated hour shall be disqualified." It is the judge's responsibility to know and enforce that particular rule. Only he may disqualify the speaker, and marks his ballot or evaluation form accordingly.

Criteria of Judgment

Just as the debater should be aware of the factors in the judging, in the setting and in his own speaking that affect the evaluation, the debater should know also about the criteria on which a debate is judged. As a matter of fact, the debater ought to be familiar with a controversy which centers around judging. Quite likely, it will touch him sometime in his debating career.

The controversy can be summed up in this question: "Should the decision be based primarily on the issues of the debate or should it be based on the skills of the debater?" To the novice debater, the differences in the two points of view may not seem vital; to the experienced tournament debater, programmed by the flowsheet, the implications are significant. The "issues" judge contends that all of the issues — the vital and inherent questions on which the outcome of the debate hinges — must be won by the affirmative to win the decision. In contrast, the "skills" judge bases his decision on a comparison of the quality of debating done by each team. He believes that debates are conducted to improve the student's speaking skills — the ability to organize, to use evidence, to handle refutation, to analyze and research a subject, to speak well. To him, a debater can lose an issue but win the debate because of superior ability.

Our study of judges' decisions shows that currently "issue" decision-making slightly predominates among those who judge at tournaments; "skills" judges rank second. Interesting, quite a few support a middle position; sometimes they are issue-focused and sometimes skills-directed, depending upon the circumstances.

The position advocated by theorists in forensics is the middle position, walking a "tightrope," so to speak, between issues and skills.

They believe that the "issues" judges conform to a computerized style of decision making in the name of fairness and impartiality or out of fear of being branded old fashioned and being excommunicated by the "in" group. The theorists uphold the middle position because to them it is in keeping with the educational aims of debate. "Issue" judges, whether they like it or not, the theorists argue, promote shoddy analysis, the use of misleading evidence and faulty reasoning, and poor delivery practices. Such judging encourages "squirrel" cases, "spreads," "flowing" and jargon, practices educationally unsound.

The controversy continues, and the debater will have to expect that it will have an impact on those who judge his debating. Whether the debater "flows" with the majority or prefers a reactionary position depends upon what he wants to gain from debate. Perhaps he should try the middle ground, to try to do both, to speak well and to win the issues, remembering as he does so that the instructional benefits occurring to him far surpass a win or loss.

As to the specific criteria used in rendering a decision, the common ones are listed next. These are derived from the most popular ballots employed by tournament directors and are the ones generally advocated throughout the nation. Hence, the debater would do well to keep them in mind as he prepares and as he debates. Remember, however, that each debate presents unique problems which a judge, whatever his abilities, cannot anticipate in advance. Thus, the criteria should be viewed as guidelines, not absolute standards of judgement.

1.   **Analysis and organization**. (a) Are the definitions of terms and the analysis and interpretation of the proposition sound and reasonable? Is "topicality" an issue? (b) Is the faculty of analysis exercised throughout, in the following-through of crucial issues? (c) Is the organization of the team case and the individual speeches clear, without being bald?

2.   **Information and evidence**. (a) Does the speaker show convincing knowledge of the question in its various phases? (b) Does he avoid both unsupported assertions and the continual citation of authorities? (c) Is there sufficient evidence without being wearisome? (d) Is evidence used effectively and honestly?

3.   **Argument and reasoning**. (a) Is the reasoning sound? Is it quick and agile? (b) Are fallacies avoided and detected? (c) Is there evidence of original thinking?

4.   **Adaptability**. Is the debater able to extemporize and effectively adapt to opponent's arguments in his main speech?

5.   **Ability in rebuttal**. (a) Is the rebuttal speech clear-cut in its attack on significant points of disagreement between the two teams? (b) Is it organized around main arguments? (c) Is there a convincing vigor and spontaneity that comes from familiarity with all phases of the question? (d)

Is significant new evidence presented, or is it merely a repetition of evidence presented earlier? (e) Does the speaker use all his time?

6. **Effectiveness in public speaking**. (a) Does the debater speak with forceful, direct communicativeness, or does he "orate?" Does the use of notes interfere with his audience contact? (b) Does he adapt, in manner and content, to opponents and the audience situation? Does he extemporize effectively? (c) Is he persuasive as well as convincing? Does he introduce variety and humor effectively? (d) Does he seem at home on the platform, in posture and gesture? (e) Does he use good diction and pronounce words correctly? Are slips due to ignorance and carelessness or to extemporaneous speaking? (f) Has he a pleasant voice? Does he use it intelligently? Does he speak distinctly?

7. **Attitude**. (a) Is the speaker courteous to opponents, chairman, audience? (b) Is he over-controversial? Is he ever willing to yield? (c) Is he cocky and bombastic? (d) Is he offensively sarcastic?

8. **Teamwork**. (a) Do the members of the team cooperate to present a unified constructive case and to assist each other in rebuttal? (b) Which team, regardless of individual "stars," constitutes the better-balanced group?

By now, we hope that our point is made: debate judging is a complex process, affected by factors not easily controlled and dependent upon the judging philosophy of the critic. Our aim in this expositon, hopefully, is also clear: to alert the debater to the complexities so that he will be more tolerant of judging and i. : negative toward those awarding him a loss. Regardless of the decisio.., .·· skill acquired by debating should serve the debater well.

Index